AIRBUS

Guy Norris and Mark Wagner

MBI Publishing Company

First published in 1999 by MBI Publishing Company, 729 Prospect Avenue, PO Box 1, Osceola, WI 54020-0001 USA

MBI Publishing Company books are also available at discounts in bulk quantity for industrial or sales-promotional use. For details write to Special Sales Manager at Motorbooks International Wholesalers & Distributors, 729 Prospect Avenue, PO Box 1, Osceola, WI 54020-0001 USA.

Library of Congress Cataloging-in-Publication Data

Norris, Guy
    Airbus / Guy Norris & Mark Wagner
    p. cm. --(Enthusiast color series)
    Includes index.
    ISBN 0-7603-0677-X (paperback)
    1. Airbus (Jet transport) I. Wagner, Mark.
    II. Title. III. Series
    TL686.A43N67   1999
   629.133'349--dc21   99-29415

All photos in this book by Mark Wagner unless otherwise credited.

On the front cover: An early-build Lufthansa A340-211 takes off from Houston George Bush Intercontinental Airport in October 1997. Air France and Lufthansa were the first to put the A340 into service in March 1993, one month before this aircraft was delivered to the German flag carrier. Note the additional twin-wheel auxiliary unit on the fuselage centerline.

On the frontispiece: One of the oddest looking aircraft ever built, the Beluga has an overall height of 56 feet 7 inches and an immense cabin volume of 49,440 cubic feet. The vast, unpressurised upper fuselage is accessed via an upward hinging door above the flight deck.

On the title page: Air France innaugurated the first services with the A320 on 18 April 1988, just under seven years after first signing a letter of intent for the small twinjet. Here one of the carrier's A320-211s taxies at Paris Charles de Gaulle in 1998 wearing World Cup colors. France was host nation for the event that year and, for the first time in its history, became world champions after beating Brazil in the final.

On the back cover: Originally ordered for Laker Airways, this A300B4-203 was delivered to Pan American in 1985 after spending two years as a "white tail." Pan Am used the A300s on its busy east coast corridor and Caribbean routes to and from Miami, where this scene was captured in March 1988.

Edited by Mike Haenggi
Designed by Dan Perry

Printed in Hong Kong

CONTENTS

INTRODUCTION

Airbus Industrie has grown from nothing to the world's second-largest commercial jetliner manufacturer in 30 years. The consortium has forced the pace of technological change in civil air transportation and welded the European aerospace industry into a cohesive global force. Perhaps above all, it has successfully challenged the dominance of the U.S. airframe manufacturers and provided airlines the world over with a valuable alternative.

Its rate of growth is nothing short of remarkable. From a fearfully slow start in the early 1970s when, between 1974 and 1976 only 18 new orders were received for the A300B, the introduction of new models has made the business skyrocket. In 1998, Airbus took a record 556 orders worth $39 billion. This was 30 percent higher in dollar value than the previous record year and represented a 20 percent rise in aircraft numbers. Amazingly, the 1998 sales tally also equaled the entire Airbus order book for the first 17 years of the consortium's existence!

Production was also ramping up at the two assembly lines in France and Germany. In 1998 a total of 229 aircraft were delivered from the Hamburg and Toulouse lines, a 26 percent rise over 1997 and representing a turnover of $13.4 billion. Deliveries for 1999 were expected to grow to around 290, with a record 317 predicted for 2000.

By 1999, the total order book was expected to exceed 3,300 firm orders valued at around $200 billion. Deliveries by the end of 1998 stood at 1,894 aircraft, and based on the current projections, the 3,000th Airbus is expected to be delivered around 2002. With an order backlog of more than 1,300 worth almost $93 billion in early 1999, the immediate future seems bright. With new narrow-body and wide-body products under study, in development or production, the longer term prospects could be even better.

Guy Norris
1999

ACKNOWLEDGMENTS

Thank you to the many Airbus Industrie people who have helped in various ways with the creation of this book. They include Adam Brown, Patrick Baudry, Bernard van Kempen, Barbara Kracht, David Velupillai, Herve Beranger, and Andrew Hugey. We would also like to thank Frog and Rosie Barker, John Bailey, Robert Frelow, Mary Hinge, Christian Kjelgaard, Alison Lau, Wai Lun, Andy Marsh, Sheila and Giles Moore, Bobby Morse, Tony Pereira, Anna Scheel, David Simenson, Erich Wagner, and Knut and Sue Wilthil. Thanks also to the staff of Flight International, including Carol Reed, Max Trident-Jones, and Paul "Babe" Lewis. Finally a big thank you, as always, to Judy, Tom, and Greg, and to our editor, Michael Haenggi.

ONE

A300: First Wide-Body Twin

The roots of Airbus Industrie go back to a hot, humid day in June 1965 when the first of a series of unusual meetings took place at the Paris Air Show. One of these meetings was between the leading European airlines, including Air France, Alitalia, British European Airways (BEA), Lufthansa, Sabena, and SAS.

All were concerned about how they could cope with the explosion in mass air travel, then growing at the astonishing rate of 15 percent a year. Group members discussed their joint requirements for a short- to medium- range "air bus," a generic term then being applied in both America and Europe to several conceptual airliner projects.

Another group also convened in the chalets at Le Bourget. This one consisted of French and German aircraft companies, which met informally to discuss possible collaboration on a joint civil program. The talks had a more profound effect on the German companies, ATG Siebelwerke, Bolkow, Dornier, Flugzeug-union Sud, HFB, Messerschmitt, and VFW. Within weeks of the Paris Air Show they formed an informal group to coordinate their study concepts

An Airbus pioneer taxies at London's Heathrow on a bright winter morning in 1991. This A300B2-1A/101 first flew in June 1974 and was delivered to Air France, the launch customer, only five days later. It was only the sixth A300 ever built and one of 23 eventually handed over to the airline. Note the raised housing for the ADF loop aerials on top of the rear fuselage.

The longer range capability of the A300B4, like this early Lufthansa B4-2C/103, made this the most popular version until the advent of the A300-600R. During its eight years with Lufthansa the aircraft was upgraded to B4-203 standard, which increased its maximum takeoff weight capability to more than 363,000 pounds. Lufthansa, Air France, and BEA strongly influenced the system design of the earliest aircraft. The first A300B flew with two different throttle locations to suit BEA, which, although it never bought the aircraft, wanted to put a moving map in the cockpit.

under the collective name of Studiengruppe Airbus, the first formal use of the title.

By this time, it was widespread knowledge in Europe that Boeing was considering a much larger aircraft project, later to evolve into the 747. American Airlines was also busy drafting its own set of requirements for an "air bus" of its own, which would be issued the following year. The requirement ultimately led to the development of both the Lockheed L-1011 TriStar and the McDonnell Douglas DC-10, the latter actually winning the airline's business.

Although dramatic passenger growth spurred these projects, none would have been technically possible without equally amazing growth in engine power. This process began three years earlier with the establishment of the U.S. Air Force's Project Forecast, a crystal ball exercise to establish and review future requirements. Data from this revealed the potential for new, more powerful high-bypass turbofans that could power much larger aircraft than anything previously conceived. This, in turn, set the ball rolling on the USAF's CX-HLS (Experimental Cargo/Heavy

Logistics System) airlifter project aimed at delivering several hundred troops and pieces of equipment directly to the front line after a trans-Atlantic length flight.

The technology for this leap in power had its origins in the USAF's Lightweight Gas Generator (LWGG) technology-demonstrator program, which began in the late 1950s. The LWGG spawned a General Electric (GE) demonstrator that became the TF39 and later evolved into the CF6 family. The same effort also led to Pratt & Whitney's STF200 and JTF14 engines, which ultimately developed into the JT9D. The P&W engine went on to enjoy a seven-year monopoly on the 747, while the GE engine won the CX-HLS competition along with the Lockheed C-5A design.

Rolls-Royce, the original pioneer of the postwar civil jet engine, had also seen the benefits of the higher bypass ratio concept. The company's Conway engine, with a bypass ratio of 0.3:1, was the world's first successful turbofan, even though at the time it

Alitalia took eight A300B4-203s direct from Airbus, the bulk of which were still flying for the carrier in 1999. One of the last aircraft to be delivered from Toulouse, I-BUSG, is pictured alongside its stablemate "Sierra Fox" at Charles de Gaulle in 1989, eight years after handover. The airline also bought several secondhand ex-Eastern A300B4s to augment its fleet.

An Iberia A300B4-120 prepares to line up for takeoff on runway 9 Right at London's Heathrow in 1990. Note the drooped leading edge, which could be set at three positions, and the leading edge fence, which improves performance by controlling spanwise flow. Tabbed Fowler flaps on the trailing edge of the wing covered 84 percent of each semi-span and increased the chord of the wing by 25 percent when fully extended.

was still known as a bypass turbojet. Rolls-Royce subsequently stepped up research into a much higher bypass turbofan and, given the rapid rise of interest in America since 1962, had embarked on a triple-shaft engine program. The company's Barnoldswick site in Lancashire was the center for many of the studies that consequently bore the initials *RB* (for Rolls-Royce–Barnoldswick).

With all this still relatively far off, the airlines were still unsure of what they wanted. In October 1965 they convened another meeting in London, and within the month, the British and French governments sat down to form a working party to try to

come up with a suitable specification. It may seem surprising that by November the Anglo-French Ministry Working Party had already produced a completed report, but the embryonic Airbus studies could not have come at a better time as far as European cooperation was concerned. The Anglo-French Concorde project was in full swing, and Germany's rush to form its Studien-gruppe (later renamed Arbeitsgemeinschaft Airbus) was evidence of its industry's wish not to be left out of this next opportunity.

The "air bus prospects" report, published in late 1965, outlined a 200 to 225-seat aircraft with a direct operating cost 30 percent lower than the Boeing 727-100 over a range of 810 nautical miles, later increased to 1,200 nautical miles. The technological quantum leap making these targets feasible was, of course, the new engines. The paper therefore suggested the P&W JT9D and RB.178 as the engine candidates. Both of these engines offered more than 40,000 pounds of thrust.

Taking a leave from their German counterparts, and encouraged by the British government, the U.K. manufacturer Hawker Siddeley (HS) formed links with Breguet and Nord of France to study new airbus concepts. The HBN group, as it was called, studied five main configurations, one of which, the HBN.100, is now seen as the first real "genetic" link in the chain that led to the

Airbus improved the A300B's hot and high takeoff performance by adding a Kreuger flap, seen clearly here at the intersection of the wing and fuselage on this taxiing Egyptair B4-203. The reinforced fin/fuselage attachment, roof-mounted ADF aerials and circular cross-section are also prominently displayed in this head-on view. The final fuselage width was decided by a team led by Roger Beteille, who later became president and chief executive of Airbus.

A300. The HBN.100 was sketched loosely around the 20-foot-diameter width of the 747 fuselage, with which it was designed to share as much commonality as possible. This gave it the capacity to take similar underfloor containers, and thus would make it more popular for mixed fleet operators. "We had been looking at double-bubble designs," recalled Airbus vice president of strategic planning Adam Brown, "then one day, we saw the first drawings of the 747 and said, 'Hey, well maybe we should do a single deck and make it circular,' which is what we did."

In early 1966 the French companies Sud Aviation and Dassualt combined efforts on a big twin design based largely on a revised version of Sud's earlier studies of a new large transport nicknamed "Grosse Julie." The revised "galion" design was adapted by the new teammates to fit the Anglo-French specification and competed directly with the HBN.100 as a result.

With interest growing in the program, the governments of Britain, France, and Germany met to iron out a proper foundation. As a result, each country elected a designated company to represent its interests. Hawker Siddeley was the United Kingdom's company, Sud Aviation became France's nominated partner and Germany's Arbeitsgemeinschaft (later to become Deutsche

A relatively rare Pratt & Whitney JT9D-59A-powered A300B4, pictured on departure from Hong Kong Chep Lap Kok in late 1998. China Airlines was one of only four airlines, along with Iberia, SAS, and Garuda to select the P&W engine, which was not offered until 1977. The result was a mammoth 90 percent market share for the General Electric CF6 engine.

Airbus scored its first major breakthrough as a world player when it won an order for 23 A300B4-203s from Eastern Airlines in April 1978. Although worth $778 million, it was far more valuable in terms of enhancing the consortium's credibility in the vital North American market. This aircraft was delivered to Eastern in 1983, and later spent time with several operators after the airline's demise in 1989.

Airbus) was ready to step into line. The HBN.100 was selected as the prime design candidate, and formal applications for funding were made to the three governments on October 15, 1966.

By now the HBN.100 had begun to grow and was configured for up to 320 seats. The first marketing brochures were drawn up, and, to round the seat size to the closest hundred, the project was named the A-300, or Airbus 300 seats. New details of the partnership were also agreed on in May 1967

when research and development costs of £190 million were to be shared 37.5 percent by Britain, 37.5 percent by France, and 25 percent by Germany. It was agreed that Sud Aviation would have design leadership of the program in exchange for Rolls-Royce developing the RB.207 to power it.

These details were cast in stone at a go-ahead meeting held between the three governments in London in July 1967. The actual launch was made contingent on the three national airlines, Air France, BEA, and

Originally ordered for Laker Airways, this A300B4-203 was delivered to Pan American in 1985 after spending two years as a "white tail." Pan Am used the A300s on its busy East Coast corridor and Caribbean routes to and from Miami, where this scene was captured in March 1988.

Lufthansa, buying a combined minimum of 75 aircraft. The aircraft continued to grow in parallel with the promised power of the RB.207. Perhaps because of this, launch orders failed to materialize as airlines worried that the A-300 was too big and the projected launch target date of June 1968 came and went without a go-ahead.

Realizing the problem, the Airbus partners scaled down the entire aircraft and, in December 1968, came out with a slightly smaller 250-seater dubbed the A-300B. Fuselage diameter was cut back to 18 feet, 2 inches (later expanded again to 18 feet, 6 inches) and overall length reduced from 176 feet, 11 inches to 158 feet, 6 inches. The reduced size also meant that more engine types could be considered apart from the RB.207, including the smaller RB.211, the P&W JT9D, and the General Electric

Twenty-six years after the first A300 rolled off this line, serial number 792 advances through the Toulouse facility toward completion for Fed Ex. The large 141-inch by 101-inch main deck cargo door denotes this late-build model as an A300F4-600R, which can carry a maximum payload of 120,700 pounds. Strangely, the F4-600R was the first Airbus to be built on the line as a freighter. Previously, all A300 freighters were built as passenger aircraft and converted to cargo before delivery.

CF6-50. In fact the original Rolls engine project was so far behind schedule by this stage that the airframe partners had already begun quiet studies of versions with U.S. engines.

In some ways this also suited the French and German marketers who were worried about stepping up the U.S. element of the A300 for marketing reasons. "We were getting into a market that was almost totally U.S. dominated, so quite deliberately we planned that everything the maintenance crews would have to work with would be U.S.-built, such as environmental control and APUs. This dramatically increased the U.S. national content by dollar value as a result. Since then, of course, things have swung back," recalled Brown.

Further work to refine the design went on, however, and by January 1969 more than 3,700 hours of wind tunnel work had been completed. Despite significant design progress, British political support for the program began to decline dramatically during early 1969. Lack of orders, uncertainty over the future of Rolls-Royce in the program and an anti-European Labour government minister of technology, Anthony Wedgwood Benn, conspired against the effort. By March 1969, the writing was on the

Another rarity seen on approach to Los Angeles International in 1996. This A300C4-620 was one of only four built and, by 1999, one of only two survivors. Three were seized by the Iraqi government after the invasion of Kuwait in 1990, and two were blown up in subsequent Allied air attacks the following February. This aircraft, clearly displaying its side freight door, was operated by the Abu Dhabi Royal Flight.

wall for Rolls-Royce, and the airframe partners had virtually selected the CF6 in its place. The result of all this was the formal withdrawal of the British government from the project on April 10, 1969.

The French and German governments were not put off by the British decision and on May 29, 1969, signed a new agreement with each taking a 50 percent shareholding. The only British involvement remaining was through Hawker Siddeley, which, as the wing design specialist, retained a role as a major subcontractor. Hawker Siddeley opted to remain with the program under its own funding, and signed binding agreements with Sud-Aviation and Deutsche Airbus to

supply main wing boxes for the prototypes, plus an option on future wing sets. Hawker Siddeley's bold decision to risk private investment in the project proved highly fortuitous. The wing provided a valuable solid source of work for the next 20 years and, more important for the rest of the U.K.'s aerospace industry, kept the door open for Britain to rejoin Airbus again almost a decade later.

Fokker-VFW of the Netherlands rushed in to fill part of the void and joined the consortium in 1969 shortly before Airbus Industrie was formally created on December 18, 1970. Earlier that year Sud Aviation had merged with other French groups to form

The 28-degree sweep of the original Hawker Siddeley–designed wing stands out in this overhead view of a Lufthansa A300-603. Although wingspan remained unchanged at 147 feet, 1 inch, the fuselage length was increased over the original B4 by 2 feet, to 177 feet, 5 inches. The increase was caused by grafting the rear fuselage of the A310 to the forward section of the original B4. The unpressurized section of the rear fuselage was actually shortened as a result, but the pressurized parallel section was extended so that the cabin was increased by two seat rows.

An American Airlines A300-605R thumps down at Miami in March 1995. American launched the -600R, a longer-range version of the -600, with an order for 25 aircraft in March 1987. The U.S. airline took delivery of its first aircraft on April 20, 1988, and put it into service the following month, mainly on Caribbean routes out of its Miami hub.

Aerospatiale and, together with Deutsche Airbus was partnered in the newly formed Airbus Industrie under French law as a Groupement d'Iteret Economique (GIE).

The French and German companies each shared 36.5 percent of the production work, Fokker had 7 percent and Hawker Siddeley 20 percent. Spain's CASA joined in October 1971, taking a 4.2 percent stake in the consortium. This reduced the Aerospatiale and Deutsche Airbus holdings to 47.9 percent each. These shares further reduced to 37.9 percent each when British Aerospace (through its 1977 acquisition of Hawker Siddeley) joined the consortium as a full partner in 1979.

Building and Flying

Construction of the prototype began in September 1969 and Aerospatiale's Toulouse facilities in France were earmarked as the site for final assembly. The aircraft remained essentially true to the original HBN.100 configuration, with a low, modestly swept-wing

Banking over the Kowloon tenements, a Thai Airways International A300B4-605R approaches the old Hong Kong Kai Tak International Airport shortly before all flights were transferred to the new Chep Lap Kok airport on Lantau Island to the west of Hong Kong Island. Thai's purchase of the -600R continued a long relationship with Airbus going back to 1974, when the number eight A300B2 was delivered to what was then Air Siam.

and twin underhung engines. The rear fuselage had been lengthened as a result of wind tunnel tests that indicated the benefits of the increased moment arm. This meant the tail could be reduced in size, thus compensating for the extra weight of the longer fuselage. The smaller tail also resulted in lower trim and yaw drag, with subsequent improvements in flight performance.

In September 1970, Air France signed a letter of intent to buy six aircraft, by now formally referred to as the A300B1. In November 1971 this was firmed up and included a

further 10 options. The aircraft was beginning to grow again, and the basic production aircraft was made five frames longer than the two prototypes. The A300B1, which began to take shape in early 1972 in Toulouse, was 167 feet, 2.3 inches long and had a maximum takeoff weight (MTOW) of 291,000 pounds. The subsequent A300B2 was lengthened to 175 feet, 9 inches (later 177 feet, 5 inches) by adding plugs fore and aft of the wing and provided room for up to three more seat rows. Powered by slightly more powerful CF6-50C engines rated at

A China Eastern A300-600R appears to be virtually threading its way through the high rises of downtown Kowloon City in this dramatic image taken in late 1997. Airbus predicted that, despite the financial woes of the rest of Asia, China's growth would continue at a fast pace. It forecast that Chinese airlines would require more than 1,300 new airliners worth $130 billion by 2017.

51,000 pounds of thrust, this was to have a MTOW of up to 302,000 pounds and carry up to 281 passengers.

The first engines were hung off the prototype in April 1972 and, following its official rollout on September 28, 1972, the aircraft, F-WUAB, made its maiden flight on October 28. The 1-hour, 25-minute flight included undercarriage cycling and basic handling checks and was proclaimed a success. The flight test effort continued trouble-free and, after the four aircraft in the program completed 1,580 flight test hours, the A300B was awarded French and German civil certification on March 15, 1974. The first production aircraft flew one month later and, on May 23, three days after FAA certification was achieved, entered service with Air France on the Paris-to-London route—the first wide-body twin to enter service in the world.

Already the requirement for more range was making itself felt at Airbus, which quickly developed the B4 version, with a

The first of up to 75 A300-600R freighters for Fed Ex, "Molly Mickler," is pictured on climb out. Fed Ex became the launch customer for the all-freighter version in July 1991 when it announced firm orders for 25, reconfirmable orders for 25, and options on another 25. This first aircraft made its maiden flight from Toulouse on December 2, 1993, and was delivered the following May after completing the certification program.

center fuel tank. The 3,000-nautical-mile range B4, with an original MTOW of 330,700 pounds, entered service with the Frankfurt-based charter carrier Germanair (later part of Hapag Lloyd) in May 1975. The first B4 was the ninth to come off the Toulouse production line, which, by U.S. standards, was still far from busy.

A crucially important early customer at this stage was Korean Air, which ordered six in October 1974, followed, after a desperate order drought, by an order for four from Thai International. By far the biggest breakthrough, however, and the deal that set Airbus firmly on the map, came in May 1977, when it leased four to its first U.S. customer, Eastern Airlines. The Miami-based airline was impressed by the operating economics

of the big twin and, on April 6, 1978, ordered 23 A300B4s and placed options on a further nine. Together with other breakthroughs in the Middle East with Egyptair, and the orders already received in Europe, the Eastern business boosted total orders to 123 by 1979, of which 70 were booked in 1978 alone.

Advanced technology was a hallmark of Airbus from the beginning, so it came as no real surprise when news of a radical new flight-deck design development emerged. Airbus was convinced that new display and automation technology would soon allow it to design out the flight engineer station from its cockpit. The resulting forward-facing crew cockpit (FFCC) was a significant innovation. The first A300B4 equipped with the FFCC made its first flight on October 6, 1981, this configuration later became commonplace throughout the industry in the following years.

The initial flight, the first by any widebody aircraft with a two-man flight crew, lasted 3 hours and 40 minutes, the last 2 hours of which were after sunset. The trials were a success and the first aircraft, a B4-200 for Garuda Indonesian, became the first of a new breed. The FFCC was based on traditional electro-mechanical instruments, but used a totally revised systems display architecture to present data to the flight crew. The concept was later taken a step further on the A300-600 with the availability of newer digital displays. The -600 flight deck was based around six TV-like cathode-ray tube screens, two in the center to show aircraft system data and two on each side to display primary flight and navigation data.

New life was injected into the A300 line in 1980 using technology developed for the first major derivative, the A310 (see chapter 2). Launched as the "world's largest twin-jet," the new version was dubbed the A300-600 and blended the best of the earlier A300 design with the considerable advances made with the A310. The rear, parallel fuselage section of the A310 was used for the new model, allowing the rear pressure bulkhead to be moved aft and two extra seat rows added to increase maximum capacity to 375 passengers. The smaller, lighter and lower-drag tailplane of the A310 was also used. A new, advanced cockpit, based on the FFCC and ergonomically designed by Porsche, was introduced, as were several aerodynamic improvements. These included a "clean up" of the wings to improve drag, most of which was achieved by the adoption of simpler flaps without tabs. Slat fences and outboard low-speed ailerons were also deleted as part of the

improvement, which resulted in a 4 percent lower cruise drag.

Airbus delivered the first A300-600 to launch customer Saudi Arabian Airlines in March 1984, after it received certification on February 29, 1984. Later in March, subsequent deliveries were made to Kuwait, which took a convertible passenger/freighter version with a cargo payload of 110,700 pounds. Both were powered by P&W JT9D-7R4H1 engines. It was not until the following March that the first GE CF6-80C2-powered version of the A300-600 flew. This model also incorporated carbon brakes and wingtip devices similar to the slightly larger units used on the A310.

An increased range version, the A300-600R, first flew in 1987 and was introduced by its launch customer, American Airlines, in April 1988. Extra fuel, housed in a trim tank in the tailplane, extended range to more than 4,400 nautical miles, with 267 passengers and 23 LD3 containers. The notion of adding tail fuel, which increased total capacity to 19,300 U.S. gallons, was again derived from the A310—in this case the longer range A310-300 version.

By the 1990s, the A300 was entering its third decade with a new emphasis on cargo duties and roles. Just like the other first-generation wide-bodies before it, the large capacity of the big twin made it an attractive cargo aircraft both as a converted airframe, or as a new build model. Although some A300 freighters had been delivered directly off the line, the first major cargo version order was finally received from Fed Ex in July 1991, when the American freight giant ordered 25 A300-600R freighters, with options on 50 more. First deliveries began in 1994. Airbus received another boost in September 1998 when UPS placed orders and options worth $5 billion for up to 60 A300-00Fs. Deliveries were due to begin in mid-2000.

Eight A300B4s await conversion to freighters at British Aerospace's Filton site in the northern suburbs of Bristol. BAe Aviation Services launched its own cargo-conversion program for the A300 at the Paris Air Show in 1995 and won significant orders from Channel Express and C-S Aviation. Others competing for the growing A300 cargo-conversion market included DASA Airbus as well as companies in Israel and South Africa. Filton's other A300/A310 overhaul and modification work has also helped make this U.K. airport into a haven for early Airbus types.

Meanwhile British Aerospace and DASA Airbus (the successor to Deutsche Airbus) began offering cargo conversions of the earlier A300B4 models. By early 1999, some 33 aircraft had undergone the freight conversion at various locations, the vast majority of them being A300B4-200s. An indication of the newfound popularity of the A300B4 freighter was revealed by the fact that 24 of the 33 had been altered in 1998 alone. Another 25 A300B4s were also scheduled for modification during 1999, ensuring that at least 58 converted freighters would be plying the skies by 2000. With the growing need for more air freight capacity, it seemed that the cargo-conversion program option alone would guarantee the presence of A300Bs around the world's airways for many years to come.

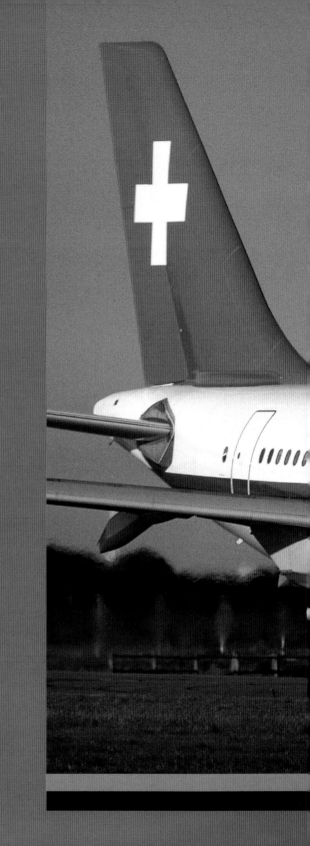

TWO

A310: Family Values

The A310 was the first major derivative of the A300 and proved that Airbus was serious about developing a family of airliners. It also boosted business at a critical period for the consortium and played a pivotal role in bringing the British back into Airbus Industrie.

The development of an A310-sized aircraft had been planned from the inception of the consortium. It had studied three major derivatives, based around the original A300 fuselage and, by 1974, had narrowed these down in three main projects. The first was a stretched, high-capacity version called the A300B9, the second a shortened variant called the A300B10, and the third a long-haul derivative with four engines dubbed the A300B11.

In 1976, facing huge development costs for any new project of its own, Boeing made a tentative approach to join forces with Airbus on the B10. The concept was called the "BB10" and it planned to combine the Airbus fuselage with Boeing wings. The wings of the A300 were the domain of British Aerospace, however, which, by this time, was anxious to rejoin Airbus as a full member. The talks with Boeing soon foundered over insuperable differences, and the American company continued with development

Swissair launched the A310 with a firm order for 10, plus 10 options, in March 1979. This aircraft, pictured lining up for an evening takeoff in 1990, made its first flight on April 1983 and was delivered the following month to Swissair. This A310-221 was later converted into a -221F freighter by ILFC, which leased it to Fed Ex in 1995.

Like other European operators, KLM bought the A310 as a replacement for its DC-9 Series 30s on major trunk routes throughout the continent. This aircraft, a -203, first flew in December 1983 and had been in service for almost 18 months with KLM when this scene was captured at London's Heathrow in 1985. Like many of its sister ships, this aircraft was plying the night skies over the United States as a freighter for Fed Ex by the late 1990s.

Lufthansa's A310 purchase was largely "home grown" thanks to the large percentage of parts made by DASA Airbus in Germany. This included the forward and upper center fuselage, redesigned rear fuselage, doors, tailcone, and the fin and rudder, the latter seen here shining like new in the crisp sunlight of a French summer day in 1989.

A hard-working Swissair A310-322 is readied for pushback from the gate at Zurich as a company Boeing 747-300 rotates on the runway behind. The A310-300 was an extended-range variant with an increased maximum takeoff weight of 330,695 pounds, and almost 2,000 U.S. gallons of extra fuel capacity. Most of this was accommodated in a tailplane tank that could be used to alter the trim of the aircraft for a more efficient cruise.

of its own 7X7 project, soon to become the 767. It had already become apparent to all concerned that the B10 variant would require a new wing if it was not to be terribly compromised, and a design team at Hatfield (where Hawker Siddeley had designed the original A300 wing) had already begun unsolicited work on a completely new design, heavily optimized toward the B10's mission.

Airbus firmed up design plans for the A300-10 in 1978, but it planned to have the new wing made by a French-German-Dutch integrated-wing design team. With airline interest mounting in the aircraft, the project was renamed the A310, and a national competition was set in motion for the best wing design. The goal was to achieve best performance with a smaller and lighter wing, and the competition set the integrated wing team against the British, who realized that winning would give them the best chance of re-entering Airbus as a full-up member. The German-led design was essentially conventional, with a deep supercritical

Although impossible to tell from the outside, the A310-300 was the first production jetliner to have a fin box made from composite materials. The first use of composites for such a large primary control surface reflected increased confidence in the manufacture and repair of the lightweight material.

section and Fowler flaps. The British wing, on the other hand, had a slightly greater thickness/chord ratio at the root but was distinctively tapered in thickness from below. This produced a marked dihedral (upward sloping) surface to the inboard, lower wing which produced low drag, good ground clearance for the engines, and provided extra volume for fuel.

As befitting a European company, the outcome was a combined wing that brought the best of the British and integrated team's design concepts together. The main structure was based on the Hatfield design, with the adoption of the German Fowler flaps outboard and "vaned Fowler," or double-slotted flaps, inboard. The vital news for the British participating in Airbus was that the wing would be built in the United Kingdom, with a large group of French and German engineers moving there to help with the design. The supercritical wing featured a 28-degree sweep, an area of 2,360 square feet, and a span of 144 feet, compared to the A300B's 147 feet, 1.25 inches. The wing also provided the incentive for a Belgian consortium, Belairbus, to join Airbus with responsibility for production of A310 slats, tracks, and Krueger flaps. It also took on manufacturing composite fairings.

As the design of the wing firmed up, so did the rest of the aircraft. The entire rear fuselage, though based on the same cross-section of the A300B, was redesigned with a longer parallel section aft. This enabled the rear pressure bulkhead to be moved back farther and increased seating for up to 237. Although shorter than the A300B by 11 frames (150 feet, 6.7 inches compared to 175 feet, 6 inches for the A300B2/B4), the

The foreshortened impression of the A310 is somehow reinforced by the Singapore Airlines paint scheme in this view of a company -222 aircraft being pushed back at Changi airport in January 1986. The cabin was 11 frames shorter and overall fuselage 13 frames shorter than the A300B2/B4.

redesign of the aft fuselage enabled a smaller, lighter tail. The vertical fin, for example, was to be made from composites representing the largest primary structure at the time ever to be nonmetallic. The aircraft was also designed with common pylons to support both GE and P&W engines, and carbon brakes were offered as standard. From 1985 onward, the later production aircraft were also distinguished by drag-reducing wingtip fences.

The A310 launched into production on July 7, 1978, on the back of commitments from Swissair, Lufthansa, and Air France for 35 aircraft. The two family members then envisaged included a regional A310-100 and a transcontinental 3,000-nautical-mile-range A310-200. The latter had a higher MTOW, a center fuel tank, and could carry 210 passengers. The first firm order for the A310 was taken from Swissair on May 10, 1979, when it announced plans to take 10

The advanced, reduced-span wing design of the A310 was a critical element of the derivative's configuration and placed the program in a different category from the simple shrink originally planned. Here the wing takes the strain as a Hapag-Lloyd -204 heads home from Palma, Majorca, with a load of sun-tanned German tourists returning from vacation in early 1990.

The A310 was the second member of the family to introduce the delta-shaped wingtip fences as standard. The devices reduced drag by preventing higher pressure air below the wingtip from flowing to the upper surface. This slowed the onset of vortex generation, thereby reducing drag and improving fuel efficiency. It also helped maintain better spanwise lift distribution toward the wingtip, further increasing cruise efficiency.

With leading-edge slats and trailing-edge flaps fully extended, this China Northwest A310 nears touchdown at an approach speed of less than 135 knots (155 miles per hour). Even at its maximum landing weight of around 270,000 pounds, the A310 could still stop in less than 5,000 feet at sea level conditions.

(plus 10 on option) to replace McDonnell Douglas DC-9-30s on its European trunk routes. Lufthansa and KLM soon followed with further orders and options for 70 and, by the end of 1979, the A310 firm order book stood at 58 with 59 more options.

This had grown to 181 orders and options by the time the aircraft made its first flight on April 3, 1982. A total of 15 airlines had signed up for the new twin, representing a world of difference from the faltering start of the A300 almost exactly a decade earlier. The orders were all for the -200 version, so Airbus stopped offering the -100, none of which were built.

French and German certification was achieved on March 11, 1983, with U.K. CAA approval for the A310 obtained in January 1984. FAA certification was granted a little over a year later in February 1985. The first delivery to Swissair was on March 25, 1983, followed within days by the first A310 to Lufthansa. The German airline put its first aircraft into service on April 12, followed nine days later by Swissair.

Stretching the Range

The long-range potential of the A310 also made it ideal as a replacement for the fleets of 707s and DC-8s then approaching

33

Although the A310's cabin was shortened by 11 frames compared to the A300, it could take proportionately more passengers because the sides of the redesigned aft fuselage were more parallel than the tapered A300 rear section. This pushed the rear pressure bulkhead position farther aft, creating room for three more seat rows and providing capacity for a maximum of 280. This Pakistan International Airlines -308, seen taxiing at Rome Fiumicino, is configured with a more normal 212 dual-class seating arrangement.

the end of their useful careers. Airbus leaped at the market opportunity, and in 1982 announced it was developing a new version called the -300. Like its contemporary, the Boeing 767, the A310-300 was destined to play a major role in the development of new extended-range twin operations (ETOPS) routes.

Externally identical to the -200, the -300's big changes were beneath the skin, where additional fuel tanks were located in the tailplane. To reduce cruise drag, the A310-300 was also fitted with a computerized fuel-distribution system. This pumped fuel around from one tank to another, depending on how much had been burnt off, and altered the trim setting of the aircraft. The finer trim control capability reduced drag, and therefore increased range by cutting fuel consumption.

The A310-300 was also designed to accommodate extra fuel tanks, called ACTs (additional center tanks) in the aft cargo hold. Each ACT could hold up to 1,900 gallons and two could be fitted. Maximum range with full fuel and 220 passengers was 5,150 nautical miles.

The extra fuel capacity of the A310-300 also meant that the structure had to be beefed up to take the extra weight. The combined effect was a range of MTOW options up to 361,600 pounds compared to the heaviest -200 weight option of around 313,100 pounds. The highest weight option, available from late 1989, was made possible by fitting the wheels and carbon brakes of the A300-600, slight structural strengthening of part of the wing, fuselage and undercarriage, and the use of more-powerful

Evening sunlight illuminates the detailed features of the redesigned wing as this Kenya Airways A310 departs from London en route to Nairobi. Although the wings retained the 28-degree sweepback of the A300, they were radically "gulled" with an 11.8-degree dihedral angle inboard, and a 4.3-degree dihedral outboard. Thickness/chord ratio went from 15.2 at the fat root to 10.8 percent at the tip. The gulling kept the engines well off the ground, but also provided more space for fuel.

The A310 became the first Western-built aircraft to be certified by the Russian State Aviation register in October 1991. Five years later it again underwent rigorous cold weather tests in Yakutsk in the Republic of Sakha, Eastern Siberia, where it was successfully restarted after a 16-hour overnight cold soak in temperatures down to minus 50 degrees Celsius. The A310 was also the first Western wide- body to be used by Aeroflot Russian International Airlines, one of whose leased aircraft is seen here on finals.

engines. The highest thrust power plants available included the GE CF6-80C2A8, rated at 59,000 pounds thrust, and the 58,000 pounds thrust P&W PW4158A.

Swissair became the first customer for the -300 when it announced on June 21, 1983, the conversion of four -200 orders. Just over two years later, on July 8, 1985, the first A310-300 made its first flight from Toulouse. Although initially powered by JT9Ds, the aircraft was later re-engined with PW4000s in November the following year. The first GE-powered A310-300 made its maiden flight on September 6, 1985. Commercial A310-300 services began in

December 1985 when the first Swissair aircraft began flying a route linking Geneva and Zurich with Cairo, Monrovia (via Dakar), and Khartoum (via Athens).

Just like its bigger brother, the A300B2/B4, the A310 began to enjoy an aftermarket renaissance as a freighter in the mid-1990s. The stimulus was again provided by Fed Ex, which launched the A310 cargo conversion in September 1993 when it acquired Lufthansa's 13 A310-200s. The first conversion, by DASA Airbus, was completed in mid-1994 and delivered to Fed Ex on July 18, 1994. During 1995, Fed Ex signed another deal with DASA to convert a further 17

By 1999 Fed Ex had become the world's largest A310 operator, with 39 in the fleet. The express freight carrier took its first A310-200, an ex-Lufthansa aircraft, in July 1994 after conversion by DASA Airbus in Bremen. Other aircraft, such as this A310 pictured on climb out from Orange County, California, were acquired from operators such as Swissair and KLM.

aircraft, all of which had been operated by either KLM, Martinair, or Swissair.

The A310 also formed the basis for new military transport and was offered by Airbus as a multirole tanker transport (MRTT). Military versions were operated by the Canadian, French, Thai, and German air forces, the latter of which bought two -300s from Lufthansa in 1996 for conversion into tankers. In its tanker role, the aircraft was designed to carry up to 77 tons of fuel. Another adaptation of the A310 was offered by Raytheon E-Systems to the Royal Australian Air Force for its airborne early-warning and control system requirement. For the RAAF's "Project Wedgetail," the A310 was offered with an Elta-made, 360-degree electronically scanned, phased array radar mounted on top of the fuselage.

Perhaps the oddest and ugliest of all A310 concepts was the "Cryoplane." This was studied by DASA Airbus as a demonstrator liquid-hydrogen-powered aircraft, and resembled the Beluga transport in appearance (see chapter 6). The liquid hydrogen was to be stored in 10-foot, 4-inch diameter tanks mounted above the fuselage within a faired-in cupola, floored with reinforced plating. To enable passenger loads to be increased to a viable 319, DASA proposed stretching the A310 fuselage by 22 frames (36 feet, 1 inch). The aircraft was expected to have a range of 2,700 nautical miles with a full load.

Production of the A310-200 ceased after the delivery of the 85th aircraft to Cyprus Airways on February 28, 1989. The A310-300 continued in production right through the 1990s, though by the end of the decade manufacturing had slowed to a trickle and Airbus began to study options for an A300/310 replacement.

THREE

A320: Family within a Family

The emergence of the A320 family did more to set Airbus firmly on the map than any previous development. Not only did it produce a range of smaller airliners on which to build a vastly larger customer base, but it provided a new focus for plans for a new narrow-body, which had kept most of the European aerospace industry frustrated for years.

The true forerunner of the A320 was a project called JET, or Joint European Transport. Set up by all the partners in Airbus, but not the consortium itself, the JET project had been stirred into life by a long succession of failures. The 1970s has seen one project after another abandoned while Boeing and McDonnell Douglas (MDC) soared ahead with their 737-200 and DC-9 programs. Victims on the road to JET included various 150-seater projects such as VFW-Fokker, Dornier, and a Hawker Siddeley study, and another 180–200 project dubbed EUROPLANE. This latter effort embraced the British Aircraft Corporation, which was looking for a follow-on to its relatively successful One-Eleven program; MBB; Saab-Scania; and CASA of

The availability of new generation high-bypass turbofans like the CFM International CFM56 spurred the development of the A320. Initial models were offered with the 25,000-pound thrust CFM56-5A1, or International Aero Engines V2500-A1. Higher-thrust versions up to 26,500 pounds were offered on later models to improve hot and high takeoff performance.

Airbus designed the double-bubble fuselage to be 12 feet, 11 inches wide, permitting six-abreast seating configurations in a relatively roomy cabin. Airbus admitted the move to go for a slightly wider cabin than Boeing's single aisle cost it a structural weight penalty, but more than paid off when it came to sales. By 1999, sales of the A320 family were approaching the 2,000 mark.

Air France inaugurated the first services with the A320 on April 18, 1988, just under seven years after first signing a letter of intent for the small twinjet. Here, one of the carrier's A320-211s taxies at Paris' Charles de Gaulle in 1998 wearing World Cup colors. France was host nation for the event that year, and, for the first time in its history, became world champions after beating Brazil in the final.

Spain. The EUROPLANE grew and grew, and it was abandoned when it began encroaching on the slightly larger A310.

One of the victims even included an unusual trans-Atlantic link between Dassault, Aerospatiale, and McDonnell Douglas. Reviving some links first established in the 1960s, this last initiative was aimed at an all-new airliner. The two companies had previously worked together to give Douglas the American sales, marketing, support, and possible manufacturing element of the Caravelle program. Fortunately for Airbus, the proposed Advanced Short/Medium Range Transport (AS/MRT) project was also abandoned. JET was created in the aftermath of the failure of AS/MRT and all the other projects, and almost immediately took on a look of what was to become the A320.

The initial JET studies focused on three family members ranging in size from 130 to almost 190 seats. The aircraft would cruise

41

A derated version of the A321's 30,000-pound thrust V2530-A5 was developed by IAE for the A320 and called the V2527-A5. Rated at 26,500 pounds, it first flew on an A320 testbed in November 1992 and entered service with United Airlines just over a year later in December 1993. United's 1992 order for the A320, which had increased to 86 by early 1999, is believed to have been one of the deciding factors behind Boeing's move to develop the Next Generation 737.

The A320 was the first airliner to go into production with a composite (carbon fiber, reinforced plastic) tailplane. This unit is built by CASA along with the elevators, mainwheel doors, and parts of the rear fuselage. The center and rear fuselage, seen here on a new aircraft at Toulouse, are built by DaimlerChrysler Aerospace Airbus. In December 1998, 29 aircraft of all types were delivered, representing the highest number in a single month in the consortium's history.

Production of single-aisle aircraft rose to 168 in 1998, a massive jump of 32 percent over the previous year. The bulk of this growth took place on the A320 line at the Toulouse site, pictured here, while the flurry of A319 and A321 orders also meant Hamburg saw its share of growth.

considerably faster than the 737 at around Mach 0.84, with a much larger range potential and it would be powered by two of the newly developed CFM International (CFMI) CFM56 engines. The high-bypass engine was already under scrutiny from Boeing for the next 737 derivative, the 737-300, and the JET team was aware that other new technology developments would be needed if the project was to make any market impact.

Around the same time, in 1980, the team also realized that the existing Airbus

structure was ideally placed to take over the JET concept studies. As a result, the SA (single aisle) study team was set up early that year at Airbus's Toulouse site under the former JET team leader, Derek Brown. Almost immediately the former JET studies assumed new titles. The smaller 130-seater was dubbed SA1, the midsize became the SA2, seating between 150 and 160, while the largest version seating up to 188 was called the SA3. Although they did not know it at the time, the SA team had unwittingly

Airbus made an important sales breakthrough to the Japanese market with the sale of A320s to All Nippon Airways. The airline took delivery of this aircraft, a -211, in November 1991 and within two years leased it to associate airline, Air Nippon.

created the "genetic" basis for what would become the A319, A320, and A321.

With such ideas still far off in the future, Airbus appeared to close off the door to the larger option early on when it decided to concentrate on the two smaller versions. The SA designation also vanished in February 1981, to be replaced by a new name: the A320. The smaller of the two new versions, the A320-100, was to be 118 feet, 3 inches long and could seat 130 to 140 passengers. The larger A320-200, at 128 feet, 9 inches, was designed to seat between 150 and 160.

The design received a new focus later that year when Delta Air Lines announced a specific requirement for a 150-seater. Virtually overnight, Airbus dropped the smaller variant and concentrated all its efforts on the larger version, which was tailored almost

precisely to the needs of Delta. The aircraft featured a slightly wider cabin cross-section than the Boeing narrow-body family, and a fuselage length of 122 feet, 9 inches. The decision cost Airbus extra weight, which it spent several years working to reduce, but more than paid for itself by winning big business. The revised design was again offered in two versions, only this time the difference was in payload and range, rather than number of seats. The A320-100 had fuel tanks in the wing only and could carry 150 passengers across ranges up to 1,860 nautical miles. The A320-200 had more fuel in a center tank and could carry the same passenger load around 2,850 nautical miles.

Further good news for the embryonic program came at that year's Paris show when Air France, the most loyal Airbus supporter

British Airways finally got around to ordering its own Airbus aircraft in 1998 when 59 A320 family jetliners were selected for its new narrowbody fleet requirement. Ironically, British Airways was actually one of the longest-serving A320 operators, having inherited the first batch of rare -100 series aircraft ordered by British Caledonian as far back as 1983. This aircraft, named "Isle of Man," first flew in 1989 and was one of five A320-111s absorbed into the fleet with the takeover of BCAL.

of all, signed a letter of intent for 50 aircraft. The order included 25 firm plus 25 options, and was split between 16 A320-100s and 34 A320-200s. Air France opted for the A320 over several other possibilities. Boeing had launched the 737-300; it was still studying a proposed 727 re-engined derivative and was discussing an advanced 150-seater design loosely called the 7-7. In addition, McDonnell Douglas and Fokker were working closely together on a new 150-seater project called the MDF100. Years later Air France eventually ordered new versions of the 737, the only survivor of all the aforementioned projects.

About the same time, Airbus took a bold and controversial decision to adopt a military style fly-by-wire (FBW) flight control system (FCS) for the A320. The decision sent a clear signal to the marketplace that Airbus was determined to bring as much new technology to the project as possible. The FBW concept, already well-proven on military fighters, had never been attempted on a new production passenger aircraft before.

It offered several advantages, including lower weight and cost. It also meant that the FCS could be tailored to suit the exact flying limits of the aircraft and provide envelope

Phoenix, Arizona-based America West was one of the first U.S. customers for the V2500-powered A320. These two aircraft, one in the original livery and the nearer A320 in the nicknamed "Jurassic Park" livery, were among 31 in operation by early 1999. The airline also had 33 A319s on order. At America West's request, IAE developed the "Phoenix Package" upgrade kit, which put A5 technology into the A320's A1 engines. This considerably improved hot and high takeoff performance as well as extending life on wing.

protection against careless handling. In addition, handling characteristics could be made similar to other family members, further emphasizing the benefits of flight deck commonality. Up until this point, the A320 would have had the A310 flight deck. With the switch to FBW, the control columns disappeared and were replaced with side stick controllers similar to those on the F-16 fighter. All subsequent Airbus flight decks followed this style.

Unlike conventional aircraft in which the controls were manually connected to the flight control surfaces, the A320's FBW system relied on five FCS computers to interpret the crew's control input and move the flight controls accordingly. Each of the five dual-channel FCS computers "kept an eye" on the others linked to its system. Redundancy was provided by making one of the dual channels active, while the other monitored the operation of the second.

A Tunis Air A320-211 displays the 25-degree sweep of the elegantly simple wing design. The onboard computers in the flight control system prevent it from exceeding the aircraft's structural and aerodynamic limitations. Even if the pilot holds the sidestick controls fully forward, it is impossible to go beyond the aircraft's maximum operating speed (Vmo) for more than a few seconds.

A Northwest A320-212 rotates smoothly at John Wayne Airport, Orange County, California, en route for Minneapolis-St. Paul. Even if the crew mishandled the unusual noise-abatement departure procedure at this California airport, the flight-control system would ensure a positive rate of climb by automatically opening the throttles and controlling the angle of attack to maintain a safe airspeed above stall. Northwest's 1986 order for up to 100 A320s was one of the most significant U.S. sales breakthroughs of the decade for Airbus.

Three computers were used for spoiler and elevator control, while the others controlled ailerons and elevators. The rudder and tailplane trim devices continued to be connected manually to the flight deck and could be used to bring the aircraft safely down in case of an FBW system failure.

The flight deck displays were also third generation. Each pilot's instrument panel was equipped with two color side-by-side Thomson CSF/VDO 7.25-inch by 7.25-inch displays. The outer display was the primary flight display, which indicated attitude, altitude, speed, and heading. The inner display was the navigation display, over which a weather radar image could be superimposed. Other unusual design features of the aircraft included a disproportionately large use of carbon-based composites. More than 8,500 pounds of composites were used for components such as flaps and undercarriage doors, as well as virtually the entire empennage.

Although the design finally firmed up, growing slightly in length as it did so to 122 feet, 3 inches, the project ran into funding troubles. Airbus required around $200 million for the development program, and it was not until March 1984 that financing was in place to allow the final go-ahead to be approved by the Airbus board. By this stage the orders had begun to come in and, at the launch date, stood at 96 from five customers. The first firm order, for seven, was placed by British Caledonian (now British Airways) in October 1983.

Mexicana was the first Latin American operator of the A320 and paved the way for significant orders in the region later in the decade. In 1998 the TACA group of Latin American airlines placed orders for up to 179 "A320 family" aircraft, the second largest in Airbus Industrie's history.

More business poured in following the firm go-ahead. Although the A320 had been launched with the CFM56 engine, it was also by now offered with the competing V2500 developed by International Aero Engines. This consortium consisted of Pratt & Whitney, Rolls-Royce, the Japanese Aero Engines Corporation, MTU, and FIAT, and was established in 1983 specifically to develop a new family of mid-size thrust engines for a variety of aircraft, including the 150-seat market. With a later development time scale, roughly a year behind the

CFM56-5 version then being offered for the Airbus, IAE claimed a significant fuel burn advantage. In November 1984 Cyprus Airways became the first customer to choose the V2500-powered A320. Pan American, which ordered 16 firm and 34 options, also selected the V2500 in January 1985, as did Inex Adria. The Pan American aircraft orders were later acquired by GPA for lease to Braniff.

By far the biggest single order for the A320, and without doubt one of the most significant orders ever placed for Airbus, came in October 1986 when Northwest Airlines

Airbus slightly extended the trailing edge of the A321 wing with double-slotted flaps, as seen clearly on this Alitalia A321-112 as it nears touchdown. The front fuselage plug forward of the wing measured 14 feet and was made by Alenia in Italy. The aft plug, extending for 8 feet, 9 inches aft of the wing, was made by British Aerospace.

signed an order for 100. The CFM56-powered aircraft were finally confirmed at the 1990 Farnborough Air Show. During 1986 it became obvious that market interest was strongest in the -200 version, so from line number 22 the -100 option was dropped. The aircraft was also given wingtip fences similar to the A310, and all aircraft were built with structural strengthening for the higher maximum takeoff weight and center section fuel as standard. This gave a maximum range of 2,865 nautical miles.

Certification and Stretching

The first A320 was rolled out through a fog of dry ice and a spectacular latticework of laser light on February 14, 1997. The A320 made its first flight at Toulouse only eight days later and proved easy to handle. Test flying proceeded smoothly, with European certification being awarded just over a year later, on February 26, 1988. In all, the four aircraft in the test program accumulated around 1,200 hours on 530 flights. The first aircraft was handed over to Air France on March 26, 1988, and the first passenger services began shortly afterwards.

With orders, options, and commitments already close to 450 at the time of rollout, the future of the A320 seemed assured, and the development of follow-on derivatives appeared to be a logical move. First off the mark was the stretched version, called the A321, which was launched in November 1989 following commitments from 10 customers for 183 aircraft. European airlines in particular had kept a close watch on the program for a proposed 180- to 220-seater which, until June 1989, was variously referred to as the "Stretched A320," A320-300, and A325.

To keep costs down, the program was aimed at minimum change, and after much internal debate, the original wing design of the A320 was left essentially unchanged for the larger model. To accommodate some anticipated performance needs, the wing was slightly changed to support a double-slotted flap and a slight trailing edge kink. The major change was to the fuselage, which was extended with two plugs to produce an overall length of 146 feet, some 22 feet, 9 inches longer than the A320.

The longest stretch was the front fuselage, which was given a 14-foot plug forward of the wing, while the aft fuselage was stretched with an 8-foot, 9-inch plug aft of the trailing edge. Four enlarged overwing exits (5 feet by 2 feet, 2 inches), were also built into the fuselage, which was strengthened in many areas to take the higher operating empty weight, which increased by 13,400 pounds to 105,000 pounds. The MTOW of the baseline A321-100 was set at 183,000 pounds, a hefty increase of 21,200 pounds over the standard A320. The stretch provided room for 24 percent more seats and 40 percent more hold volume, putting the aircraft within reach of the lower end of the 757 market.

To meet airline requests for more range, Airbus soon raised optional MTOW to 187,400 pounds, giving it a range of 2,350 nautical miles with 185 passengers. This was still 400 nautical miles less than the

Reverse thrust, flaps, slats, and spoilers slow an Air Macau A321-131 seconds after touchdown at the newly opened Macau International Airport in the fall of 1997. By early 1999, Airbus predicted that the Chinese market would require more than 1,380 new jetliners to cope with the growth expected by 2017. Of this total, some 711 were expected to be in the 70–175 seat category, which was straddled by its "A320 family" and A318 aircraft.

With an overall length of 146 feet, the A321 was around 9 feet shorter than the Boeing 757-200 with which it competed, particularly in Europe. Swissair was operating 10 A321-111s on intra-European routes by 1999. The airline equipped its fleet with the CFM56-5B2 engine fitted with specially developed, double-annular combustors. These reduced emissions of several pollutants, particularly nitrous oxides.

A320 and considerably less than the 757. Although this was not such a vital factor in Europe, where trunk routes are generally shorter than in North America, Airbus once more studied further growth. The result was the A321-200, which was launched with an order from Aero Lloyd via ILFC, in March 1995. The first aircraft was delivered in April the following year and started service in May 1996. The -200 featured an increase in MTOW of 13,200 pounds to 196,200 pounds. Together with increased thrust engines and 766 gallons of extra fuel in an additional center tank (ACT) in the rear cargo hold, the range was increased by up to 400 nautical miles, to around 2,750 nautical miles.

The A321 also marked other important changes for Airbus. To help finance the estimated $480 million development costs, Airbus entered the International Bond Market in 1991 at the time of a major Eurolira bond issue. Managed by Banco di Napoli and Lehman Brothers International, the issue raised sufficient capital to cover the bulk of the costs. Additional funds were also raised through a $180 million loan facility from the European Investment Bank, as well as through another set of private investors. The innovative financing arrangements resulted, in part, from lessons learned during the agonizing few years of fighting to finance the A320.

Another significant development was the opening of a second production line by DASA Airbus at Hamburg to build the A321, and later the A319. DASA originally pushed to have a second A320/321 line opened at Hamburg and a bitter dispute erupted between the French and German partners. The French argued the move would cost up to $150 million in unnecessary expenditure, while the Germans claimed the new line would be more economic and productive for Airbus as a whole. Although national pride was thinly disguised throughout the episode, it was finally resolved when the construction of a purpose-built line was authorized for A321s at DASA Airbus's Finkenwerder plant in Hamburg. In addition, the Aerospatiale contingent agreed that A320s would fly to Hamburg to be fitted out with interiors following assembly at Toulouse. Together with the later launch of the A319, which was also allocated to Hamburg, total production at the German site was expected to reach 11 per month in later years.

Shrinking a Derivative

Through the late 1980s, several of the Airbus partners began independently studying new 80- to 130-seater projects to attack the growing regional jet arena and provide a new generation successor to early DC-9s, 737s, and One-Elevens. In 1990, Airbus itself began studying the possible development of a smaller A320, dubbed the M7 (minus seven seat rows), which would tackle the same market and provide it with a direct competitor for the 737-300/500 for the first time. It would also give Airbus something with which to challenge the new MD-95, which McDonnell Douglas announced at the 1991 Paris Air Show.

The birth of the little Airbus was, however, fraught with difficulties. The issue of

Lufthansa's first A319-114, D-AILA, approaches London's Heathrow in fine weather during the summer of 1997. Shortened by seven fuselage frames compared to the A320, the A319 was assembled in Germany alongside the A321. By 1999, Lufthansa was Airbus Industrie's largest single airline customer, with 164 aircraft in service or on order, 20 of which were A319s. This biggest customer overall was leasing giant ILFC, with 281 orders.

where it should be made was again a source of dispute between the French and Germans. DASA proposed that the A319, as it was then being called, should be built at the new Finkenwerder site alongside the A321. In addition, it proposed that the A320 line should be transferred to Hamburg. The furor was solved when it was agreed the A319 would be

United followed up its A320 fleet order with the purchase of up to 48 A319-131s, one of which is pictured on final approach. Note the brightly colored spinner inside the inlet of the aircraft's IAE V2524-A5 engines. Maximum takeoff weight with these engines, each rated at 23,500 pounds of thrust, was a creditable 149,910 pounds.

built alongside the A321 but that the A320 should be left in situ in Toulouse.

Another problem was initial opposition to the project from Aerospatiale, which thought the A319 would compete with a proposed "Regioliner" family then being studied with DASA. The German company, however, was already losing interest in the study and pledged its support to the new Airbus project. DASA later became a major shareholder in Fokker, and all independent studies of 100-plus-seater projects were funneled into the Fokker 100. British Aerospace meanwhile promised to scrap its own plans for a twin-engined version of the 146 called the New Regional Airliner if the A319 went ahead.

These "political and interpartner differences," as Airbus put it, delayed the planned launch decision from March 1992 to May 22, when the supervisory board finally announced the start of a marketing campaign. Despite optimism that the A319 would be formally launched at that year's Farnborough show in September, the big

orders failed to arrive and the campaign extended into 1993. Airbus had managed to secure firm orders for six A319s from ILFC, but decided it needed larger commitments before launching the $275 million development program.

With rumors of large orders in the wings from Swissair and Alitalia, Airbus finally gave the go-ahead to the A319 program on June 10, 1993, the opening day of the Paris Air Show. As expected, the aircraft was defined with a 12-foot (7-frame) shrink, giving it an overall length of 111 feet. The shrink was achieved by removing a 63-inch plug forward of the wing and an 84-inch plug aft of the wing. Wingspan remained unchanged at 111 feet, 10 inches, though the inboard spoilers were deleted and the engines were derated to 22,000 pounds and 23,500 pounds of thrust. Some system changes were made, including an alteration to the flight control system to adapt it to the shorter moment arm of the smaller fuselage. The rear cargo door was

The stocky appearance of the shortened A319 is apparent in this view of a United -131 running up to full power as it prepares for takeoff from Orange County's John Wayne Airport in California. The A319 was cut back to 110 feet, 11 inches, in overall length, compared to the A320's 123 feet, 3 inches.

also modified, while the bulk cargo door was removed altogether.

Final assembly of the first A319 began on March 23, 1995, at the Hamburg site, and it was rolled out on August 24. The aircraft, serial number 0546, made its first flight the next day, marking the start of a 350-hour flight test program involving two aircraft. The first version, powered by CFM56-5B6/2s, was certified in April 1996, while the qualification of the V2500 (V2524-A5) powered variant started the following month.

Swissair took delivery of the first A319 in a ceremony at Toulouse on April 25, 1996, and put it into service by the end of the month. The stubby Airbus broke a world record in January 1997 when an A319 on a delivery flight to Air Canada flew the 3,588-nautical mile great-circle route from Hamburg to Winnipeg, Manitoba in nine hours, five minutes.

More derivatives were studied, including a business aircraft variant dubbed the A319CJ (Corporate Jet). This was a direct response to Boeing's launch of the BBJ version of the Next Generation 737 and was aimed at

capitalizing on the A319's slightly wider cabin. With specially fitted long-range fuel tanks, the aircraft was configured to fly up to 6,300 nautical miles.

The first version, now called the Airbus Corporate Jetliner (ACJ), rolled out of the Hamburg factory in October 1998 and by January 1999 was fitted out with the extra tanks and an array of flight-test instrumentation. Flight tests were due to begin in Toulouse in May 1999, with certification expected around midyear after a 70-hour program. The test effort focused on the performance of the more powerful engines and the higher operating ceiling of 41,000 feet.

Deliveries of the first ACJ were scheduled to begin in November 1999 after outfitting at a VIP completion center. By early 1999, Airbus had amassed orders for 12 ACJs.

On April 15, 1999, Airbus was able to celebrate the delivery of the 1,000th and 1,001st A320 family aircraft in a double event in France and Germany. Aircraft 1,000, an A319 for IFLC, was rolled out of the renamed DaimlerChrysler Aerospace Airbus assembly line at Hamburg. The 1,001st was an A320 delivered from Toulouse to United.

FOUR

A330/A340:
Twin Aisle Tactics

Bigger and longer range derivatives of the original A300 were planned from the very beginning and were to reach their ultimate expression in the form of the A330 and A340. These two aircraft were so closely related that Airbus treated them as a single program. The only significant difference between these extraordinarily interlinked aircraft was the number of engines.

The roots of both reach back into the early 1970s when Airbus began sketching out two A300B derivatives, the B9 and B10. The B9 was a stretched version of the A300B2 and could seat around 320 by accommodating an extra six rows. The B10, on the other hand, was a shortened version of the original Airbus and was designed to seat around 220. Market demand accelerated the development of the shorter version, which was eventually launched in 1978 as the A310.

The evolution of the B10 concept sparked interest in a new derivative, dubbed the B11. This was studied as a long-haul, medium-capacity aircraft with a B10-based fuselage and larger wings. The aircraft was essentially aimed at the 707 and DC-8 replacement

Airbus Industrie engineering test pilot and former astronaut Patrick Baudry's favorite Airbus cavorts around a late summer English sky over Farnborough in 1998. Baudry commanded the A330-200 for its maiden flight in August 1997 and ranks it, along with the A320, among the best handling Airbus models he has flown. Here the Rolls-Royce Trent testbed aircraft is pictured on display, three months after its maiden flight in June 1998.

With the Sacre Coeur, Mont Martre, and the Eiffel Tower providing a classic Parisian backdrop, the prototype A340-311 prepares to display its remarkable agility at Le Bourget in June 1997. This longer fuselage, -300 version was the first A340 to fly, making its maiden flight in October 1991. The shorter -200 variant joined the flight test program the following April.

market and envisioned a 180- to 200-seater with a range of up to 6,000 nautical miles. The newly available CFM56 engine seemed the right solution, so this was adopted as the baseline power plant.

In 1980, following the launch of the A310, the partners redesignated the B9 and B11 projects as the Twin-Aisle TA9 and TA11 respectively. Some designers at Airbus were concerned about the relatively limited power of the CFM56 engine, so a trijet version was also studied. The trijet TA11 was outlined with Rolls-Royce RB.211-535s or Pratt & Whitney JT10-232s (later to become the PW2000), but studies came to nothing. CFM International meanwhile convinced Airbus that it could provide more power and lower operating costs with its smaller engine.

Just as the trijet idea was waning, Airbus conceived the master stroke of developing both aircraft around a common wing. The move was largely the brainchild of Airbus chief engineer Jean Roder. He created a common wing structure with the four-engined version's outboard power plants providing bending relief moment to counteract the increased weight of the longer range version. With only minor local changes, the same wing could therefore be fitted with only two engines for the medium-range twin or four for the long hauler. The common wing dramatically cut development costs and, in effect, provided the breakthrough Airbus needed to launch the entire program.

Adam Brown, who described the design as ". . . a piece of brilliant insight" added that "if

The tall main gear of the A340 seems to reach out for contact with the ground as this Virgin Atlantic Airways -311 soars overhead on short finals. Virgin became an enthusiastic A340 operator and even took delivery of the second and third prototypes in April and May 1997, respectively. The airline also became a launch customer for the stretched A340-600.

The second prototype A340-311 completed flight tests and, following refurbishment, was sold to Virgin Atlantic, which put it into service in April 1997. The aircraft, construction number 002, is seen turning on finals for Hong Kong's Kai Tak airport the following December.

you took exactly the same structure, you could use it to get more lift by hanging the outboard engines further out. You could do all this without compromising the aircraft for either longer range or shorter range missions."

Full go-ahead for launch was still a few years away, however, and Airbus remained busy just defining the two products. Both began to grow in capacity and range in the early 1980s and became more focused on the Lockheed L-1011 and McDonnell Douglas DC-10 replacement market. By 1982, the TA9 was outlined as a twin with a 27-feet, 9-inch stretch over the A300. This enabled it to seat up to 410 in all-economy, but still burn 22 percent less fuel than a

contemporary trijet. The TA9-100 version was capable of flying 1,500 nautical miles while the heavier -200 was aimed at sectors up to 3,300 nautical miles in length.

The TA11, was defined as a quad jet, able to carry around 220 passengers over long ranges of up to 6,800 nautical miles. At the 1982 Farnborough Air Show, Airbus revealed it was also studying a twin-engined derivative of the TA11 called the TA12, which had a similar payload, but a range of 5,000 nautical miles.

Airbus spent the next three years slowly gathering momentum to proceed with a launch. By 1985 the designs had altered again and the TA12 disappeared altogether from the program. The TA9 and TA11 emerged with a raft of advanced technology features transferred directly from the A320. This included the fly-by-wire flight control system, side-stick controllers, and the advanced digital flight deck. Going one step further, Airbus also outlined a variable camber wing, which was designed to basically change shape in midair. The computerized system made slight adjustments to the trailing-edge flaps to optimize the cross-section for different phases of the cruise. The advanced wing concept never made it into production and was dropped on cost grounds.

The fuselage of both versions was also redefined at this stage with a length of 194 feet, 10 inches, some 17 feet, 5 inches longer than the A330. Internal debate still raged at Airbus, however, over the number of engines needed for the TA11. Roder's design breakthrough had given it the flexibility to offer both, but the real question was,

The prototype A330 now flies for Cathay Pacific. Built as a -301, the prototype made its first flight on November 2, 1992, powered by General Electric CF6-80E1s. In late 1993, it was fitted with Rolls-Royce Trent 772s and converted to a -342. On January 31, 1994, it became the first Airbus aircraft to fly with Rolls engines and, after certification, was delivered to Cathay in October 1996. It is pictured decelerating after landing at the new Chep Lap Kok International in November 1998. In the background, an army of workers race to complete construction of the second runway, which was due to open the month after this shot was taken.

what did the airlines want? To answer this, the newly appointed Airbus managing director, Jean Pierson, put together a focus team to study the issues. The outcome revealed the majority of airlines were in favor of a quad layout, though virtually all the North American operators leaned toward a big twin. Asian airlines, on the other hand, were equally unanimous in their support of the quad, while Europe was divided on the subject. The use of twins on long overwater, or ETOPS routes, was still in its infancy at the time.

With a clearer idea of market demand, the Airbus Supervisory Board met in January 1986 and renamed the two aircraft. The TA9 became the A330 and the TA11, the A340. Airbus initially planned it the other way around because customer interest was clearly stronger in ordering the quad jet first. The designations were reversed at the request of the sales team, however, after it argued that airlines would make more sense of a quad jet if it had a *4* in its name, rather than a *3*.

The A330 was now defined with capacity for 308 passengers and a range of 5,800 nautical miles. The A340 was outlined with a range of more than 6,700 nautical miles and space for 261 passengers. In October 1986, Airbus followed up on its six-year-long pledge to CFMI and signed a memorandum

Some A340s were quickly pressed into service as executive or VIP transports. The Sultan of Brunei and the Qatar Amiri Flight were among those who purchased models. Here a Qatar-owned A340-211 climbs out of Meecham Field in Fort Worth, Texas.

The first A330-321 delivered to Thai Airways International taxis past the main passenger terminal at Hong Kong's Kai Tak in November 1996. The Pratt & Whitney PW4164-powered aircraft is configured with 50 business-class and 265 economy-class seats. Problems with the thrust reverser delayed delivery until December 1994.

of understanding with the company over the use of the CFM56-5S1 as the baseline engine for the A340. This was essentially a 28,000-pound thrust "throttle push" version of the A320's CFM56-5A1 and was right at the lower end of the required thrust margin.

Still, the configuration was far from fixed for either version. At around the same time as the A340 engine agreement, Airbus announced it was stretching the A330 by 10 feet, 2 inches to seat an additional 24 passengers. The A340 was also defined with a center section auxiliary undercarriage leg like the DC-10-30 and MD-11. This was to allow operations from low bearing strength runways, and the center gear was also made an optional feature on the A330.

In late 1986, International Aero Engines (IAE) approached Airbus with a surprise offer. Desperate to counter CFMI's lead, it had come up with an ultra-high bypass (UHB)

version of the V2500, dubbed the SuperFan. This featured a variable-pitch single-stage fan driven through a gear system by the V2500 core. The SuperFan not only offered better than adequate thrust levels of 30,000 pounds plus, but it also offered dramatic fuel savings of more than 17 percent over the V2500 and even more over the CFM56.

This had tremendous repercussions on range and payload predictions, giving Airbus new room to outperform its direct rival, the MD-11. The baseline A340 was hurriedly re-defined as the A340-200 which could fly 7,850 nautical miles with 262 passengers. A new stretch, called the A340-300, was also announced. This would be capable of carrying 295 passengers over 7,000 nautical miles and was 14 feet longer than the -200.

CFMI rushed to make a comeback in the face of the SuperFan threat and proposed the CFM56-5C1 with 30,000 pounds of

An early-built Lufthansa A340-211 takes off from Houston's George Bush Intercontinental Airport in October 1997. Air France and Lufthansa were the first to put the A340 into service in March 1993, one month before this aircraft was delivered to the German flag carrier. Note the additional twin-wheel auxiliary unit on the fuselage centerline.

thrust. This new rating made it the highest power engine yet attempted by CFMI and featured an added booster stage, an improved exhaust mixer, and higher temperature-resistant materials to cope with increased operating temperatures.

The promise of higher power engines effectively kick-started the market into action. On January 15, 1987, Lufthansa announced it had board approval to buy 15 SuperFan-powered A340s and place options on a further 15. The twinjet marketers also saw signs of new life, and two months later Air Inter placed the first orders for the A330 when it selected 5 firm and 15 options. At the same time, Thai International also placed orders and options for 8 A330s. Airbus wrapped up a triumphant month when, later in March, it revealed a letter of intent from Northwest Airlines covering orders and options for up to 30 A340s.

Ten days after the Northwest deal, just when it seemed nothing could go wrong

with the program, Airbus suffered a serious setback. IAE abruptly canceled the SuperFan, saying it was "premature to launch in the light of the technical program risks of meeting an entry into service date of spring 1992 to satisfy the airline's desires. The SuperFan concept is not in question and engineering evaluation for a variety of applications will continue to be pursued." Ironically, it was to be another Airbus project 11 years later that would offer the first stepping-stone toward the rebirth of something similar to the SuperFan: Pratt & Whitney's geared fan PW8000 project (see chapter 5).

The cancellation of the SuperFan was a huge blow to the A340 sales force, which immediately sought assurances from CFMI that it would somehow boost performance to fill the power gap. Airbus itself helped by immediately increasing the wingspan from 183 feet, 9 inches to 192 feet 3 inches and adding 9-foot-tall winglets in place of the original A310-style wingtip devices planned.

CFMI, meanwhile, came up with a 31,200-pound thrust version called the CFM56-5C1. Ultimately it began offering a 34,000-pound thrust version called the -5C4 from 1995 onwards.

Despite launch orders for both the A330 and A340, formal go-ahead was held up until partner funding was secured. The program got the official green light on June 5, 1987, just before the Paris Air Show. By this stage total commitments had reached 98, of which 38 were for the A330 from three customers and the remainder for the A340 from four customers.

With the program now moving swiftly forward, Airbus announced a few more last-minute changes to the A330, which was stretched by another 3 feet, 7 inches to make it the same length as the A340-300. The aircraft was renamed the A330-300 and could seat another seven passengers. Over the same period, BAe completed design definition of the wing, which was 40 percent larger than that of the A330. New deals were also struck with all three of the big engine makers. General Electric, which was the first to be offered on the A330, planned a higher thrust variant of the CF6-80C2 later called the -80E1. Pratt & Whitney offered the PW4164, while Rolls-Royce developed a new, higher thrust version of the RB.211-524 called the "L," which later evolved into the Trent 700. This marked the first occasion on which airlines had been offered a choice of all engine makers on an Airbus.

Despite the Lufthansa, Air Inter, and Thai orders from the year before, none had formally signed firm contracts, and it was not until June 13, 1988, that a firm customer—the King of Spain—signed for an A340. This was followed later that year by firm orders for both the A330 and A340 from Los Angeles–based leasing company ILFC.

A330s come together in the giant Clement Ader assembly building. All the various subassemblies arrive ready-made from the partners and are snapped together at Toulouse. This system ensures that partner companies maintain total responsibility for major parts, rather than simply becoming subcontractors.

Without engines it is virtually impossible to tell the A330 apart from the A340; however, the Korean Air A330-300 and its nearby stablemate can be differentiated by the positioning of the inboard engine pylons.

The order rate for both big jetliners was much lower than Airbus wanted, partly because of direct competition from the MD-11. The A340, in particular, was offered in head-to-head competition, and for a brief period in 1988 Airbus and McDonnell Douglas held exploratory talks over cooperative ventures that would be mutually beneficial rather than destructively competitive. The talks ranged from an MDC variant of the A320 to replace the MD-80 to an MD-11 fuselage with an A340 wing. The discussions collapsed during the year, however, and the two returned to open competition in markets around the world.

One of the key battlegrounds was the tiny island of Singapore, whose prestigious airline, Singapore International Airlines (SIA), was looking for a long-haul wide-body smaller than the 747-400 to service its European routes. MDC, anxious to secure much-needed new business for its big trijet, grabbed what seemed like the final victory in 1990, when it won orders for 20 from SIA. Over the next few months as the MD-11 entered its flight test program, however, it became depressingly clear to SIA and MDC that the trijet was simply not up to the mission. SIA had given the manufacturers the job of meeting the worst-case scenario: Singapore to Paris with a full load against prevailing westerly winds in midwinter in the northern hemisphere. With the results MDC was getting from flight tests, the MD-11 would run out of gas somewhere over the Balkans and major improvements were needed.

SIA demanded solutions and, in desperation, MDC presented the airline with a

Engineers run through avionics checks as an A330-300 nears completion. Note the side-stick controllers, just visible at both sides of the flightdeck, and the six multifunction EFIS displays. The flightdeck is virtually identical to that of the A340, with the obvious exception being the number of throttle levers. The flight decks are so similar across the range of recent Airbus products that the FAA and JAA approved cross-crew qualification for the A320, A321, A330, and A340.

last-minute wing redesign with supplementary short-term fixes like long-range fuel tanks in the belly cargo hold. The wing redesign was so sudden that SIA had no warning of it from the manufacturer until it was revealed to the airline's chief executive over dinner. The ill-judged move gave Airbus the chance it was looking for. Sensing SIA's increasing anger and frustration with MDC, Airbus sent a team from Toulouse and presented the case for an extended-range, high gross weight version of the A340 called the A340-300E. SIA liked the proposal and on August 2, 1991, promptly canceled the MD-11s and ordered the new A340s instead.

The turnaround marked the beginning of the end for the MD-11 and, worse still, contributed to the ultimate demise of MDC itself some six years later. Conversely, it marked the end of the beginning for the A340, firmly establishing the credibility of the long-range Airbus in the crucial Asia-Pacific market.

First Flight

Due to the greater market demand for the A340, and the -300 in particular, it was this version that flew for the first time on October 25, 1991, just 21 days after rollout from the specially constructed Clement Ader final assembly facility in Toulouse.

The big aircraft, the largest civil jetliner ever made outside the United States, successfully completed a 4-hour, 47-minute maiden flight, marking the start of a fast-paced test effort. The first short fuselage A340-200, serial number 004, joined the test program on April 1, 1992. European

Kuwait Airways' first A340-313 soars overhead on climb-out. The aircraft was delivered in March 1995 as part of the airline's reequipment program following the decimation of its fleet during the Gulf War four years earlier. Control of the A340 in pitch is maintained by a trimmable tailplane and separate left and right elevators. The tailplane can also be controlled mechanically from the flight deck, with FBW computer inputs superimposed. Slats and flaps are controlled outside the main FBW complex by duplicated slat- and flap-control computers.

A Garuda A330-341 nears touchdown on Runway 13 at Hong Kong's Kai Tak airport. The A330's ailerons automatically droop with full flap selection and can deflect 25 degrees up with spoilers to dump lift after touchdown. Within a few seconds, the crew of this aircraft will hear a voice warning that demands throttle closure at 20 feet during the landing flare.

The lengthened forward fuselage section of this Cathay Pacific A340-313 is well illustrated in this angle during climb-out from the new Hong Kong Chep Lap Kok airport. The -300 is 208 feet, 10 inches in overall length, compared to 194 feet, 10 inches for the -200.

JAA certification was received on December 22, 1992, following a 750-flight, 2,500-hour test program involving six aircraft.

All was not perfect, however. The test flights revealed some worrying performance deficiencies, and with lessons of the MD-11 experience still fresh in the memory, Airbus and CFMI embarked on a rapid series of airframe and engine improvements.

By March 1992 Airbus had outlined a series of improvements to the wing that it hoped would yield a 1 percent drag reduction. Although this target seemed insignificant in a general sense, it represented a huge goal for the aerodynamicists, for whom drag improvements are normally measured in one-tenths of 1 percent. The consortium was therefore relatively pleased when the improvements resulted in a 0.7 percent yield, rather than the 1 percent target. The work at

CFMI meanwhile produced some significant improvements in fuel burn. A continuous improvement program instituted by the engine maker recovered a 1.5 percent fuel burn by the end of 1992 and a further 2 percent by the end of 1994. Other means of reducing drag were also explored in due course and included tests of a low-drag skin film called riblets, rear fuselage strakes, increased wing incidence, and a change in the thrust vector of the outboard engines.

There was some good news, however, when Airbus discovered that the overall airframe weight was 1,100 pounds lighter than expected. In addition, fuel volume was found to be around 1,660 U.S. gallons greater than the original specification, and takeoff performance was better than predicted. As a result, the A340 was offered with additional fuel options and was certified with an increased

Egyptair's first A340-212, SU-GBM, approaches London's Heathrow at the end of its flight from Cairo. Approximately 13 percent of the wing is made from composite materials, including the outer flaps and flap track fairings, ailerons, spoilers, leading-edge fixed surface panels and winglets.

takeoff weight of 566,580 pounds against the original 558,900-pound target.

February 1992 also saw the start of major assembly of the first A330, which was also the 10th airframe on the combined production line. Tests on the static airframe began and were going well until September, when news leaked out of a failure in the rear spar. At first it seemed Airbus's seemingly brilliant common wing concept was in danger of being fatally flawed. After BAe investigated the failure, however, the airlines and Airbus breathed a sigh of relief when it was discovered that only the A330 was prone to the problems, which were relatively easy to fix.

The first A330 rolled out on October 14, 1992, and flew for the first time on November 2. The 5-hour, 15 minute flight passed without incident and led to a virtually trouble-free certification program that culminated in simultaneous JAA and FAA certification on October 21, 1993. The 12-month, 1,100-hour flight test effort also revealed that performance was better than anticipated, and the A330 could carry an additional 6,600 pounds of payload on sectors of 3,000 nautical miles.

Lufthansa had taken delivery of its first A340, a -200, on February 2, 1993, while Air France received the first A340-300 the following May. Airbus also managed to squeeze in one more milestone for the year by delivering the first A330 to Air France Europe (the former Air Inter) on December 30, 1993. The aircraft entered service on the airline's busiest domestic route between Paris and Marseilles on January 17, 1994.

Flight testing of the PW4168-powered A330 was meanwhile under way at Toulouse and going well until disaster struck on the afternoon of June 30, 1994, when the test aircraft, F-WWKH, crashed on the airfield. The tragic loss of the aircraft and its seven crew members led to a complete revision of flight test procedures at Airbus and highlighted the need for careful monitoring of the A330's speed during autopilot/altitude capture operations. The crash had occurred during tests at maximum aft center of gravity, minimum speed, and maximum angle of climb, and involved the simulated failure of one engine.

The impressive wings of the A340 take the strain as this Egyptair aircraft lifts off. British Aerospace completed its 2,000th set of wings for Airbus in early 1999. It took 21 years to deliver the first 1,000 from the first set it delivered (as Hawker Siddeley) in November 1971, and only seven years for the second 1,000. Based on the 1999 order book, it expected to deliver the 3,000th set in 2002.

A Pratt & Whitney PW4168-powered A330-322 belonging to Korean Air lines up for takeoff at Kai Tak in November 1997. Nosewheel steering is used, as seen here, to maneuver at slow speeds, but it automatically disengages in favor of rudder control above 100 knots (115 miles per hour).

A brace of Dragonair A330-342s in action at Hong Kong. To protect the A330 from tail scrapes, the sensors on the aircraft automatically begin to restrain nose-up pitch demands if they exceed 4 degrees per second when the aircraft nears the ground.

The P&W-powered A330, which was certified only 28 days before the accident, had more trouble in store. Deliveries were delayed several months while problems were corrected with the composite-made thrust-reverser assembly. Thai International, which was originally due to take its first aircraft in September 1994, finally got the aircraft that December. Malaysia, which likewise was due to take its first aircraft in August, eventually took delivery in February 1995. Problems were not isolated to the P&W version. The first GE-powered A330 delivered to a North American operator was forced to divert on its inaugural flight due to an oil leak while the Rolls-Royce Trent 700 fleet was temporarily grounded due to bearing failures in the gearbox.

These incidents were unusual, however, and the certification programs for all versions were otherwise straightforward. Rolls-Royce began to make up for 25 years of lost opportunities with Airbus on January 31, 1994, when the first Trent 700-powered A330 made its maiden flight from Toulouse. The aircraft was actually the first prototype, but had its GE engines replaced with the British power plants for the test program. Flight tests were completed with two aircraft, one belonging to launch customer Cathay Pacific, and the Trent version was certified on December 22, 1994, after 500 hours of tests. Initial services began on February 27, 1995, from Hong Kong, marking a new chapter for Cathay Pacific, Airbus, and Rolls-Royce.

A China Eastern A340-313 makes its escape from the crowded Kai Tak ramp. The sheer volume of traffic, and the resulting propensity for wide-bodies, made the Asian market a fertile hunting ground for the Airbus sales team. The consortium predicted that more than 670 wide-bodies will be needed by Chinese airlines alone to cope with the expected boom in traffic by 2017.

Even as the third and last version of the initial A330 family was completing certification, plans for new derivatives were already underway. The intimate relationship between the two models was amply demonstrated at this point. Airbus had already begun to beef up the structure of the A340-300 to meet the long range and high weight requirements of SIA. The spin-off benefits became available to the A330 team, which used the strengthened wing and additional fuel capacity to develop a new long-range version to counter the 767-300ER. The resulting A330-200 was 10 frames shorter than the -300 and was launched in November 1995. With seating for 380 in all-economy and a range of 6,500 nautical miles, the A330-200 provided airlines with a perfectly sized, new-generation replacement for the DC-10-30.

The first -200, powered by GE CF6-80E1 engines, made its maiden flight in August 1997 and was jointly certified by the FAA and JAA.

The consortium aimed it squarely at "the more active long-haul market." To emphasize this renewed assault, Airbus also took the opportunity to offer an ultra-long-range A340 model called the -8000. This denoted the variant's 8,000-nautical mile range, which enabled it to fly non-stop from either U.S. coast to Hong Kong. Additional belly tanks were carried to provide a total fuel capacity of 43,100 U.S. gallons. Together with higher structural weight, this extended the A340's maximum takeoff weight to 606,300 pounds, compared to just under 570,000 pounds for the initial -200.

While the A340-300E provided a bridgehead to the -8000 and A330-200 developments, Airbus knew the basic design was capable of much more. Static and fatigue

73

Airbus made several minor aerodynamic changes to improve the performance of the initial A340 design, including adding 10 percent to the chord on the outboard portion of the number one (inboard) slat to relieve wave drag. It also considered raising the height of the nose leg to reduce the nose-down attitude at parking stands, though this was later considered unnecessary. By 1999 it was also testing other low-drag initiatives, such as a hybrid laminar flow system on an A320 tailfin, which could eventually be introduced throughout the family.

tests from 1991 to 1994 demonstrated the depth of the design's inherent structural reserves, and shortly after these were completed, BAe began studying new ways of increasing wing area to take advantage of this. Previous A330/340 stretch studies had simply traded range for payload, but with the revised structure and BAe's wing work, Airbus could suddenly look seriously at more significant growth.

Key to the new wing design was a root insert, which increased chord, span, and wing area and provided an extra 25 percent fuel volume. The larger wing box also required a three-frame stretch of the center fuselage, thereby providing the baseline dimensions for the initial variant. At the same time, the wing span was also enlarged with 5-foot tip extensions, creating an overall wing area some 20 percent larger than that of the basic A340.

Two new derivatives were planned around the enlarged wing, the ultra-long-range A340-500 and the higher capacity A340-600. Both would be powered by new engines in the 50,000-pound to 60,000-pound thrust class. By this stage in early 1996, all three of the big engine makers were

The bright tail feathers of a Philippine Airlines A330-301 provide a vivid splash of color against the drab olive backdrop of the hills around Kowloon as the aircraft makes the tight turn onto finals at the old Kai Tak airport in late 1997. Note the prominent 9-foot-tall winglets.

To improve the range of the high gross weight A340s like this Air Mauritius -313, Airbus introduced a slight wing twist to alter incidence angle and also realign the engine thrust vector. This longer-range A340-300 is capable of carrying 295 passengers over 7,300 nautical miles.

Pleased with the performance of its A340-313 fleet, Air Canada later became one of the main driving forces behind the development of the A340-500/600 effort. By 1999 it had 13 A340s in service or on order.

suffering from the high development costs and low-margin returns of successive campaigns for the A330 and 777. All three therefore wanted an exclusive deal with Airbus such as that enjoyed between CFMI and Boeing on the 737. Of the three, GE came up with the best offer, and in April 1996 it signed an exclusive agreement to study a proposed new engine for the duo called the GEXX.

The deal was short-lived, however, and after a sometimes acrimonious dispute over risk and cost sharing, the parties fell out in February 1997. Rolls-Royce and Pratt & Whitney immediately fought to replace GE and, at that year's Paris Air Show, the U.K. company emerged as the victor with a new engine called the Trent 500. Rated at between 56,000 pounds and 62,000 pounds thrust, it combined a scaled down Trent 800 core with a new low-pressure turbine, and the 97.5-inch-diameter fan and low-pressure systems of the Trent 700. The smaller core, combined with the large fan, produced a very high bypass ratio of 8.5, which was expected to lead to high efficiency and low noise, particularly on takeoff and approach.

At the same time as the deal was signed with Rolls, Airbus was careful to point out that P&W was still in contention and that the agreement with the U.K. manufacturer was therefore not strictly exclusive. The P&W engine was the PW4557, which combined features of the PW4000 versions developed for the A330 and Boeing 777. Pratt & Whitney also aimed the hybrid engine at the increased gross weight 747-400 and 767-400ER.

Simultaneously with announcing the engine decision, Airbus also gave the go-ahead for the commercial launch of the derivatives. The full go-ahead for the $2.5 billion aircraft program came in December 1997, by which time some 100 commitments had been secured from seven customers, including the earliest to show interest, Virgin Atlantic and Air Canada. At the time, the consortium was confident that the A340-500/600 could capture at least half of the 1,500 sales in the category forecast through to 2010.

The A340-500, powered by the Trent 553 version, was envisaged with a basic three-frame stretch over the A340-300,

The larger Rolls-Royce Trent 500 turbofan will immediately help differentiate the A340-500 (right) from its A340-300 forebear. The extra stretch of the -600 (left) will make identification of this derivative even easier. The Trent 500 is due to be flight tested on an A340-300 testbed in 2001.

thanks to the larger wing root size. It was designed to carry around 310 passengers over ranges up to 8,500 nautical miles at cruise speeds up to Mach 0.84. Combined with the new wingbox and the increased center fuselage section, the -500 had 48 percent more fuel capacity than the -300.

The A340-600, on the other hand, was outlined with a 20-frame extension, making it more than 30 feet longer than the -300. The huge jet was capable of carrying 378 passengers, in a tri-class layout, over ranges of up to 7,500 nautical miles. The increased maximum gross takeoff weight of more than 800,000 pounds also required a four-wheel center main undercarriage unit in

place of the original two-wheel gear. This model had roughly 38 percent more fuel capacity than the -300.

By late 1998, production of the first parts for the A340-600 began at Aerospatiale's Nantes facilities, where the first metal was cut for the wing center section. The timetable called for the first flight of the -600 in January 2001, followed by the -500 in July 2001. Deliveries of the -600 were scheduled to begin early in 2002, with the first -500s following shortly after. With commitments for the family standing at more than 130 by 1999, it looked as if the A340-500/600 was going to double the order book and give the 777 more than a run for its money.

FIVE

Large and Small: A3XX and A318

As Airbus approached the end of the century, and its third full decade of manufacturing, the consortium focused its attention on new developments at opposite ends of the capacity scale. At the top end was the massive A3XX, a double-deck behemoth that Airbus hoped would finally end Boeing's dominance with the 747. At the lowest end was the diminutive A318, a 100-seater to challenge Boeing's 717-200.

Airbus always recognized that it could only really hope to compete effectively with Boeing if it could offer a complete family of comparably sized aircraft across the full capacity range. Following the go-ahead of the A330/A340 models in the late 1980s, it therefore began to focus on the next big challenge: an advanced technology competitor to the 747. There was more than just pride at stake. Market forces were driving Airbus toward a larger aircraft family, and the case for such an expensive and risky venture seemed overwhelming.

The world's major air routes were booming, economic growth was accelerating in key market areas of Asia-Pacific, and airport slot congestion at large hubs was pointing the way to the need for larger aircraft rather

Some idea of the general interior layout of the mighty A3XX can be grasped from this computer-generated cutaway. Note the large, double-width stairway in the forward section and the between-deck location of the flight deck. *Airbus*

By late 1998, wind tunnel tests of the A3XX were in full swing at the British Aerospace Airbus low-speed wind tunnel in Bristol. Note the pronounced dihedral, or upward sweep of the wings of this 1/28th-scale model. *Airbus*

than increased frequency of flights. Major carriers like British Airways, United, SIA, and Japan Air Lines all voiced interest in a new generation jumbo with up to 15 percent lower direct operating costs than the 747-400.

Airbus initially began looking at 600- to 800-seat designs under a generic program called the Ultra High Capacity Airliner (UHCA). In 1991, it began definition of requirements by talking to some key 747 operators. The results generated a two-family approach with a smaller version capable of carrying 600 in a three-class arrangement, and a larger version able to seat up to 800. Many intriguing shapes were studied to meet the requirement, including fuselage cross-sections that were ovoid, horizontal double-bubble, circular, and even clover-leaf. For a while, the most promising appeared to be a fat, wide fuselage that was created by mating two A340 cabins side by side. The two were to be faired over, forming a high-capacity oval cross-section.

A key task of the design team was to keep the UHCA small enough to operate from existing airports. It would be no good building a massive airliner that could only use a handful of airports around the world. Several discussions were held with a range of airports and a consensus reached on the upper limits for length, wheelbase, and wingspan that would allow the use of existing taxiways, runways, gates, and aprons. The result was a baseline UHCA with a wingspan of 255 feet, 10 inches and an overall length of 260 feet, 2 inches. The upper limit was the 800-passenger version, with a span of 275 feet and a fuselage 265 feet long.

In accordance with span limits later adopted by the International Civil Aviation Organization (ICAO) and the FAA for their "Code F" and "Group VI" standards, respectively, Airbus later defined the upper size limit as 262.5 feet. Similarly, the overall length limit was also capped at 262.5 feet after recommendations from ACI, the Airports Council International. The result was the "80m" box, which internationally defined in metric and also used as a guide by Boeing.

Not satisfied with its own studies of essentially conventional configurations, Airbus also worked with a Russian design institute on a flying wing seating anywhere from 550 to 900 passengers. Studies of the 340-foot span tailless aircraft, dubbed the FW-900, were later terminated. Interestingly, the studies coincided with work by McDonnell Douglas, and later Boeing, on a similar flying wing concept called the Blended Wing Body.

Boeing also continued with work on a future airliner. Most of the studies were grouped under the collective banner of the New Large Airplane (NLA) program. They included all-new designs as well as derivatives with strong links to the 747, but all were aimed at a size category either below, or on a par with, the UHCA. Boeing's studies covered a lot of ground, including projected costs. By 1992 the company was becoming increasingly convinced that a successful NLA would require more resources than it could muster, so it decided to seek out partners and immediately encountered a major dilemma.

The only other U.S. company with the necessary experience and background was McDonnell Douglas; however, MDC's Douglas Aircraft Company was in the middle of a program to develop its own challenger to the 747, the MD-12. This left the big four European aerospace companies, Aerospatiale, British Aerospace, CASA, and DASA, as the only other options. All four were, of course, also the main partners in Airbus, but as the consortium was a GIE and not a formal company in the traditional sense, this allowed Boeing to challenge the unwritten rules in a new way. It recognized that there was nothing Airbus could do to prevent any of its partner companies from joining forces with an outsider on other projects.

Sensing an opportunity, Boeing therefore came up with a bold plan in January 1993 and asked all four to contribute to a feasibility study of a Very Large Commercial Transport (VLCT). The group's official charter was to study the possibility of forming a consortium to develop, produce, market, sell, and support a VLCT. The group, which specifically excluded Airbus, examined the market requirements for a VLCT capable of carrying 550 to 800 passengers over ranges of between 7,000 and 10,000 nautical miles.

The joint study was headed by two project directors: Jurgen Thomas of DASA represented the Europeans, and John Hayhurst led the Boeing contingent. The two chaired regular meetings that were held alternately in Europe and America. Airbus, through its partners, meanwhile exerted pressure to be involved first as an observer and then in its own right. In March 1994, Airbus officially became part of the study, which was extended to mid-1995.

In July 1995 at a meeting in Long Island, New York, the team completed the second phase of its study. It found that the VLCT was technically feasible but estimated the market was "insufficient to launch the program." The team split up for the last

The compact, double-decker configuration of the A3XX contrasts sharply with the slender appearance of the A340-500/600 derivatives, as graphically represented in this shot of display models at the 1996 Farnborough Air Show.

time and the airlines watched anxiously to see what would happen.

Boeing returned to NLA and 747 derivative studies, eventually opting for the latter as its best solution for the airline's needs. Airbus immediately refocused on a refined UHCA concept called the A3XX, which it had already initiated as an in-house study. Throughout 1995 and 1996, the A3XX design was further honed down to a two-decker with an ovoid fuselage cross-section. By adopting this compact configuration, Airbus believed it could contain the overall

size of the A3XX within the size limits earlier identified for the UHCA, yet still provide up to 40 percent more passenger capacity than the 747.

The search for partners outside the traditional Airbus family continued, but success in Asia was limited because most of the local companies seemed more interested in working on smaller projects like the proposed AE-100 program, so instead Airbus signed up a group of European-based companies for its initial partners. By early 1999 these included Italy's Alenia, Belgium's Belairbus,

A 1/32nd-scale model of the A3XX undergoes slow-speed analysis in the low-speed wind tunnel at DASA's Bremen research facilities. The large leading-edge slats, flaps, and drooped ailerons are well illustrated in this view. *Airbus*

Eurocopter, Finavitec of Finland, Fokker (Stork) of the Netherlands, GKN Westland of the United Kingdom, Hurel Dubois and Latecoere of France, and Saab of Sweden. Airbus aimed to eventually sign up enough risk-sharing partners to take between 35 and 40 percent of the program, which it originally estimated at around $8 billion overall. This was later to rise to around $10 billion with the inclusion of all factory retooling costs. Most of the new partners seconded staff to the Large Aircraft Division, which was formed by Airbus early in 1996 under the leadership of VLCT veteran Jurgen Thomas.

In late 1996, Airbus gathered together 13 major airlines in the medieval city of Carcassonne in southern France, to view its proposals, following the completion of the concept definition phase a few months earlier. The proposed A3XX family consisted of two main members, with various subvariants and derivatives. The baseline A3XX-100 was designed for ranges of 7,650 nautical miles with a capacity for 555 passengers, while the slightly larger -200 was aimed at higher-capacity routes of roughly the same range, but with around 100 extra seats. Based on these two platforms, Airbus sketched out a short-bodied A3XX-50/50R with seats for 481 and a range, in the case of the -50R, of up to 8,750 nautical miles.

Another variant was a long-range variant of the -100, called the A3XX-100R. This combined the long distance capability of the -50R with the original seat capacity of the -100. It also studied plans for a -100C Combi with a capacity for up to 11 freight pallets, 421 seats, and a 6,970 nautical mile range, as well as an all-freighter -100F version, which could carry a 331,000-pound payload some 5,725 nautical miles. Other proposed derivatives also included lighter, short-range -100S/200S models for high-capacity trunk routes such as those within Japan.

The A3XX will be the world's first twin-deck, twin-aisle aircraft. The wide cross-section will have an external diameter of almost 23 feet, creating ample space for two aisles even on the upper deck, as seen here in this Airbus cabin mock-up. *Airbus*

All versions were configured with the same 261-foot, 10-inch span and 79-foot-tall fin height, with length being the only external variable. The short-bodied -50 was outlined with a 222-foot, 10-inch length, while the baseline -100 was 239 feet, 6 inches long. The stretched -200 was an impressive 260 feet, 4 inches long. Max takeoff weight ranged from 1,190,000 pounds for the -50 and -100 to 1,285,000 pounds for the longer range -100R and stretched -200. Maximum payload reflected these differences. The -50 offered a capacity of 161,000 pounds, the -100 and -100R were designed for up to 187,000 pounds, while the -200 grossed out at 209,000 pounds.

All this load was carried on a lower cargo deck and two wide passenger decks—the A3XX being the first jetliner to reach this stage of development with a double-deck, twin-aisle

cross-section. The upper deck on the -100 was designed to carry up to 102 business-class passengers up front in a six-abreast layout, and up to 103 economy-class passengers in an eight-abreast layout. The main deck, in some layouts, was configured with first-class seating for 22 and a much larger area for up to 328 economy passengers.

Large stairs fore and aft connected the two decks. The forward dual stairways opened onto a reception area that looked more like a hotel lobby than the interior of an aircraft. Some designs even envisioned reception and check-in-type desks in the lobby area to help speed up the boarding process and direct passengers to their seats. The lobby provided access to the lower and upper passenger decks as well as to the flight deck, which was designed to sit on a "mezzanine" split-level area between the two main deck levels. Using this well-spaced layout, Airbus believed the A3XX could be turned around in the same time, or less time, than a 747-400—a critical airline requirement.

"Airlines have made it very clear to us that we will have to make the A3XX offer things that the 747 does not," said Airbus vice-president Adam Brown. "It will have to have more space and comfort, but the crucial thing is to have a turnaround time the same as the 747. So we have got to have double flow on the main and upper deck." The target was 90 minutes for 550 passengers.

Other unusual features of the design included the impressive undercarriage, with up to 24 wheels. The design combined the configurations of several aircraft ranging from the A340 and MD-11 to the 747 and 777. The main gear consisted of two wing-mounted trucks with six wheels on each bogie, two main body-mounted trucks with four wheels on each bogie, and a center-mounted gear post with two wheels. A two-wheel nose gear was also outlined, though other studies indicated the possible use of a four-wheel unit on a single axle, similar to the Lockheed C-5.

While the pace of the A3XX accelerated, Boeing surprised the industry in December 1996 by scrapping its 747-500X and -600X stretch plans. Boeing said the market was simply inadequate to justify the launch of the estimated $7 billion program, while Airbus flew in the face of this argument by remaining staunchly confident in its A3XX proposals. The consortium remained confident that there was a need for more than 1,400 aircraft of more than 400 seats through 2016. Airbus was, if anything, encouraged by Boeing's actions. Not only did it apparently clear the field for Airbus with the new technology, but it meant the A3XX's entry into service in 2003 and onward would give airports more time to prepare facilities.

The subsequent collapse of the Asian market and other factors, however, led to some changes in the A3XX plans. In early 1998 Airbus revealed that it had decided to delay the aircraft's entry into service by at least nine months, to the third quarter of 2004. Part of the reason was that it had not been able to achieve "a step change in operating economics" that it was seeking over the 747-400. It also faced the huge costs of developing the A340-500/600 derivatives at roughly the same time. This had been expected to dovetail, rather than clash, but the delay over the final engine choice had pushed the launch date back to the end of 1997 (see chapter 4).

In spite of the uncertainty, Airbus knew its long-term future was intimately linked to the A3XX. Speaking at the 1998 Farnborough show, the newly installed Airbus chief executive, Noel Forgeard, said, "There will be a demand in the next 20 years for over 1,300 aircraft larger than 400 seats, worth more than $300 billion, or 25 percent of the total revenues of the aircraft manufacturers. We simply cannot afford to let a market of this importance continue to be monopolized by our competition. The A3XX is vital to the continued welfare of Airbus Industrie."

Under the revised timescale, the consortium planned to begin making firm offers to airlines in 1999, followed by a firm launch later that year. Flight testing was due to begin around mid-2003, with entry into service around 15 months later. But even this was too optimistic and by 1999, the continuing pressures on the marketplace, particularly in Asia, added to unrelenting development work on the A340 derivatives, forced Airbus to once more set back the clock on the A3XX. The new in-service target date of late 2005 may have been later than most at Airbus wanted, but with Boeing apparently unwilling to commit to a competing design, the

85

Some idea of the 48-foot difference in overall length between the A3XX-100 and -200 can be gathered in this view of models on display in 1996. Note the AE316 and AE317 models, which were superseded by the A318 project in 1998.

consortium was still optimistic of overall success. "It's going to be the biggest commercial program ever run by anyone, and there are going to be a lot of tremendous opportunities created because of it," predicted Brown.

Mini Airbus

As Airbus pondered the future of what would be the world's largest airliner, it was simultaneously preparing to begin work on its smallest project yet, the A318. The tangled roots of the little Airbus go back to 1993 when four Asian countries began discussing the possible creation of an Airbus-like consortium to create a 100- to 130-seat airliner.

Nothing substantial came of the meetings between the four nations, China, India, Singapore, and South Korea, but the level of interest stirred up a five-year frenzy of international projects and agreements

that would ultimately lead to the A318. One of the leading proponents was China's AVIC (Aviation Industries of China), which held talks with Japan in 1994 about participation in the latter's long-running YS-X regional jetliner project. With no real progress made, AVIC then talked to the South Koreans about a joint venture. The Koreans were highly interested in being involved and formed themselves into the Korean Commercial Aircraft Development Consortium, in which Samsung Aerospace was the leading company.

News of the growing interest in the regional jet study reached Europe, and during 1994, Aerospatiale signed an outline agreement with Samsung covering a joint study. The agreement was nonexclusive, as Boeing had, by then, already signed a similar agreement with the Koreans. The picture became even more complicated the following year when, in March 1995, DASA and Samsung Aerospace announced plans to study the development for a 100- to 120-seat jetliner.

The plans were formalized in a memorandum of understanding signed on March 6, 1995, by senior DASA, Fokker, and Samsung management. The previous December, DASA and AVIC signed a similar agreement, and, through its new MoU with the Koreans, DASA appeared to be taking the lead in developing a cohesive new team.

Still, the true situation remained complex as Samsung and its partners were still talking to Boeing and McDonnell Douglas about possible joint ventures, while Alenia and British Aerospace joined forces with Aerospatiale on the back of the French company's existing agreement with the Koreans. The three European companies had earlier formed the AI(R) partnership, and during 1995 the French pushed for a unified bid to China and South Korea over a possible small jetliner program.

Progress on the project was held up because of disagreements between the Asian partners as to where the aircraft should be built. AVIC wanted final assembly at Xian, while Samsung was looking for something to fill its production site in Korea, with the prospect of licensed-F-16 assembly finally coming to an end. The Chinese held the trump card in the talks because the domestic market for the aircraft was estimated at around 250, compared to just 40 for Korea. The dispute culminated with KCADC pulling out of the program, to be replaced by Singapore Technologies Aerospace, and the renaming of the aircraft as the Asian Air Express, or AE-100.

AVIC, meanwhile, had to decide between Boeing and AI(R) as its international partner, the agreement with DASA having apparently fallen foul of the closer ties the German group had with the Koreans. The Chinese chose the AI(R) group, which quickly set up Aero International Asia to oversee its participation when an MoU was signed with AVIC in June 1996. Throughout the rest of the year it became clear that AI(R) wanted to increase European participation in the project to around 38 percent. The most obvious way to accomplish this was by involving Airbus, thereby providing an avenue for companies such as DASA and even Alenia to enter in a more substantial manner.

In March 1997, Airbus set up Airbus Industrie Asia (AIA), which had 62 percent Airbus and 38 percent Alenia ownership. By this action, Airbus effectively took over AI(R)'s role in the program, which was now tailored toward an 85- to 100-seater range and an in-service date of 2002. An MoU was signed between AIA, AVIC, and Singapore Technologies in Beijing on May 15, 1997, covering the eventual development of a family of jetliners. The first planned product from the $2 billion development was a 95- to 105-seater called the AE316, with a 115- to 125-seater called the AE317 following close behind with an in-service target of 2003. The entire program was called the AE31X.

The aircraft would be built in China with an advanced flight deck common to the A320 family. The engine contenders included the CFM56-9, Rolls-Royce BMW BR715, and Pratt & Whitney's new PW6000. This was a simple engine based on the XTC-66 core developed by P&W for the U.S. government's Integrated High Performance Turbine Engine Technology (IHPTET) effort and had fewer parts and lower weight than similar engines in its thrust class. More important for the long-term future of P&W, the enginemaker hoped to use the PW6000 as a springboard from which to launch a follow-on engine called the PW8000. This would be a geared fan engine, using the same core as the PW6000, and it formed the vanguard of P&W's planned attack on the CFM56's market stranglehold.

The partners planned to begin predevelopment in 1998, but some hurdles remained that were to prove insurmountable. These included technology transfer issues between the partners, as well as work-share details. The prospects for making headway seemed to grow worse with each successive meeting. By early 1998, Airbus revealed that it was considering making a move into the 100-seater using its own A320 as the basis. The tentative project, dubbed the A319M5 (minus five fuselage frames) came to light at the Singapore Air Show in February 1998 when the AE31X effort was already faltering. By the Farnborough show in September, the AE31X was dead and Airbus unveiled its new entrant, the A318.

Powered by the 20,000- to 23,000-pound-thrust PW6000, the aircraft was in fact 4.5 frames shorter than the A319, with an overall length of 104 feet and a wingspan of 112 feet. The smaller cabin was sized to seat 107 in two classes, and extended the A320 family down into direct competition with the 737-600 and 717-200 for the first time. Priced at around $36 million, it was some $5 million less than the A319 and $2 million below the 737-600, but $3 million more than the 717.

The A318 would be made by removing 1.5 frames from the forward fuselage and three frames from the aft. A small dorsal fin would also be added to counter the reduced moment arm of the short coupled body, and the reduction in size also meant the cargo doors had to be made smaller. This meant the aircraft could not use the containerized cargo system developed for other family members. The result was lower weight, but the A318 was still heavier than its direct competition.

A total of 109 orders and commitments received from customers including Air France, Egyptair, ILFC and TWA convinced Airbus Industrie to formally launch the A318. Sharing the same fuselage width as the other members of the A320 Family, the A318 offers the same comfort standards available on the larger Airbus Industrie single-aisle aircraft. It also shares the A320 Family's modern fly-by-wire flight controls, allowing all types to be operated by the same flight crews and maintained by the same engineers. *Airbus*

Due to enter service in the last quarter of 2002, the A318 will carry 107 passengers in a standard two-class layout up to 2,000 nm (3,700 km) in its baseline version, and will be the smallest member of the highly successful A320 Family. Over the next 20 years, Airbus Industrie forecasts a demand of more than 1,300 aircraft in the A318 size category. *Airbus*

Two months after revealing the aircraft for the first time at Farnborough, Airbus received the first breakthrough when International Lease Finance Corporation signed an MoU for up to 30 A318s. The deal, which called for first deliveries to begin in late 2002, was particularly significant since it was won in head-to-head competition with the 717. Boeing still believed ILFC could eventually order the 717, but Airbus said the U.S. leasing giant had taken "a corporate decision to select the A318" as its 100- to 120-seat offering in its portfolio. ILFC president Steve Udvar-Hazy said the move "reflects the market's preference for efficient, new technology aircraft that are members of an integrated family of common products."

The following month, in December 1998, Airbus received another boost when TWA announced a letter of intent to acquire the A318 as part of a much larger purchase of up to 150 Airbus aircraft. The deal covered firm orders for 50 A318s and 25 A320

"family" aircraft, as well as options on a further 75 Airbus single-aisle aircraft. Curiously, TWA also ordered 50 firm and 50 option 717-200s as part of the same announcement. The airline said the shorter-range 717s would be used on hub-and-spoke operations out of its main bases at Kansas and St. Louis, whereas the A318s would be dedicated to longer range services. The airline's urgent need to re-equip with modern aircraft, however, also meant that the earlier availability of the 717 played a part in its decision to buy both types.

With commitments for at least 80 A318s in the bag by early 1999, and Pratt & Whitney putting its full weight behind the development of the PW6000, Airbus duly gave the go-ahead for the industrial launch of the program later that year. Together with the expected go-ahead of the A3XX, the development of the A340-500 and A340-600 and the launch of the A318 therefore ensured that 1999 would become a milestone year for Airbus.

SIX

Guppy and Beluga: Uniting Europe

Airbus Industrie owes its existence to a unique air-transport network. This was created specially to carry huge subassemblies from the partners to the final assembly lines at Toulouse and Hamburg and ranks as the most heavily used outsize air cargo operation in the world.

The difficulties and huge cost of bringing the parts together by surface transport was demonstrated during the assembly of aircraft number one, the fuselage of which was trucked to Toulouse. "It is impossible to say how many telegraph poles and bridges would have needed to be knocked down," said Brown. "The idea to bring in parts by air really wasn't obvious at first, but it was a brilliant concept." Brown attributed it to former production director Felix Kracht. The system fostered care and attention at every stage. "The people who built the parts loaded them very carefully, and the people who unloaded them were the guys who had to make them fit. That way everybody made sure they did the best job, Brown explained.

For the first 25 years, the foundation for this system was the bizarre Super Guppy, a

A Super Guppy loads the wings for a future A320 into its voluminous interior on a miserable day at Manchester in 1996. Note the enlarged wing root, which added 15 feet to the wingspan of the Super Guppy, taking it to 156 feet, 8 inches in total. The fat old aircraft could manage 290 miles per hour at a push, but was dramatically slowed by head winds.

One of the oddest-looking aircraft ever built, the Beluga has an overall height of 56 feet, 7 inches, and an immense cabin volume of 49,440 cubic feet. The vast, unpressurized upper fuselage is accessed via an upward-hinging door above the flight deck.

heavily modified Boeing Model 377 Stratocruiser/C-97. These unusual, dramatically bulbous-looking aircraft were perfect for the job of transporting the large fuselage and wing sections to the Toulouse line with more speed and cost-effectiveness than any mode of land or sea transport. All the Airbus Super Guppies were based on an original conversion developed in the early 1960s by On-Mark Engineering of Van Nuys, California, for Aero Spacelines Corporation. This company required an outsize transporter to carry large sections of Saturn rockets from the U.S. West Coast to Cape Canaveral (now

Kennedy Space Center), Florida, where they would be "stacked" on-site.

The success of the original 377-PG (Pregnant Guppy) conversion led to the production of eight more modifications. The first of these was designated as a 377-SG, or Super Guppy, because it was larger than the basic PG version and used the higher powered Pratt & Whitney T-43 turboprops, stronger wing, and fuselage of the YC-97J testbed aircraft. The creation of the Super Guppy became, in retrospect, one of the most ironic developments in aerospace. It was originally developed for two U.S.

A set of wings is disgorged from the second Beluga directly into the Airbus final assembly facility at Toulouse. The Beluga has a maximum payload capability of more than 100,000 pounds compared to less than half that for the Super Guppy. The height of the open loading door is 55 feet, 1 inch, but the height to the sill of the loading door is only just over 16 feet. The cabin has an internal usable length of slightly over 123 feet, of which 70 feet is fully cylindrical.

wide-body programs, the DC-10 and L-1011 TriStar, and was used initially to transport DC-10 fuselage sections to Douglas, and TriStar wings from Nashville to Palmdale for Lockheed. The real irony was that the Super Guppy was essentially a Boeing aircraft, which meant that every Airbus until 1995 began life in the belly of a Boeing!

The 377-SG was fitted with a new center section that added 15 feet to the wingspan and added an extra 31 feet to the overall length compared to the standard 377. Cargo up to 25 feet in diameter could be loaded through a hinged nose, which swung out of the way to permit the payload to be loaded.

To allow the nose to swing, the nose gear was derigged to pivot like a castor some 90 degrees to one side. Jacks were also lowered under the forward fuselage to take the strain,

and the entire nose section—complete with cockpit—swung to one side on its own nose wheels. The nose gear itself was taken straight from a 707 to enable the 377-SG to cope with the stress of the often nose-first touchdowns that were quite characteristic of the Stratocruiser.

The first of two Super Guppies built for Airbus at Santa Barbara, California, flew first on August 6, 1970. Unlike the original Super Guppy conversion, the Model 201 version was re-engined with 4,912 shaft horsepower Allison 501-D22C turboprops, and combined some C-97 components as well as some Stratocruiser parts. The giant fuselage was easily large enough to swallow whole sections of fuselage and the 90-foot-long A300B wing set, making it ideal for the consortium's needs. The second Super Guppy for Airbus made its maiden flight on May 6, 1973, and was soon busy shuttling around Europe.

Wings were flown in from the United Kingdom, while fuselages from DASA and other parts traveled from Hamburg to Toulouse while others flew to the Airbus factory via Aerospatiale's Saint Nazaire and Nantes sites. Aerospatiale made forward fuselage and nose sections for the A300 and A310, and later the nose and center fuselage parts of the A330 and A340. The Guppies brought in CASA-built tail sections and doors from Spain.

With the increasing workload following the build-up of the A310 line, the two Super Guppies were seriously overworked, and Airbus began looking for new capacity. The Super Guppy was the only aircraft in the world that could realistically handle the task, but the Aero Spacelines company had been acquired by Tracor, which was not in the Guppy conversion business any longer. The need was desperate, so Airbus acquired the plans for the modification and gave them to Union de Transports Aeriens (UTA), which performed two further conversions in France. The two "new" Super Guppies joined the Airbus fleet after their first flights in 1982 and 1983, respectively.

The four aircraft soldiered on throughout the 1980s, but by the end of the decade it became obvious that with the introduction of the new A330/340, the aging Super Guppies would need to be replaced from 1995 onward. A study was conducted and all options were considered, including road, rail, and sea links. However, Toulouse was not conveniently located for anything other than air transport, and since there was no question of Airbus relocating its main production center, the consortium began the search for a new airlifter. It looked at the Antonov An-124, the An-225, Boeing 747, Lockheed C-5, and McDonnell Douglas C-17. It also looked at conversions of the 767, Ilyushin IL-86, A300B4, and A300-600R.

None of the aircraft was large enough, and Airbus did not want to perform expensive redesign on any of the parts just to make them small enough to be carried on the new freighter. The company therefore decided to make a special conversion of an existing twinjet and narrowed it down to the 767 and the A300-600R. Although the final choice of the A300-600R was not very surprising, Airbus said it was chosen after concerns that Boeing would not supply "enough technical information" for the 767 conversion.

In 1991, a new consortium called SATIC (Super Airbus Transport International Company) was formed by Aerospatiale and DASA, the two companies that bid the winning solution based on the A300-600R conversion.

The resulting A300-608ST (Super Transporter) was one of the strangest looking aircraft ever designed. Named "Beluga" after the outsized breed of sturgeon fish, the aircraft differed from the Guppy in having a lowered underfloor cockpit. This allowed an upward-opening cargo door that could not only be opened much faster, reducing turnaround time by at least 45 minutes, but that also allowed loading and unloading in winds of up to 30 knots and more. The Guppy's large movable nose slowed turnaround time because all the flight controls, hydraulics, and electrics had to be disconnected every time, and then reattached and adjusted before flight.

The first Beluga was taken from the A300-600R production line in Toulouse when it had reached the wing-center fuselage mating point. The unfinished airframe then went to Sogerma's own hangar at Colomiers, adjacent to the Airbus site at Toulouse. There the DASA-built rear fuselage and Aerospatiale nose sections were added,

The distinctive droop snoot of the Beluga has given rise to the nickname "anteater." The A300-600ST is the only unpressurized aircraft ever made by Airbus, apart from the flight deck section, and can fly at Mach 0.7 (484 miles per hour) for almost 1,000 nautical miles.

and the job of creating the bulbous fuselage began. The floor was also strengthened to take loads of up to around 100,000 pounds. To compensate for the aerodynamic blanking effect of the body on the tail, a larger A340 fin with a 4-foot root plug and a dorsal fin was added. In addition, auxiliary fins made by CASA were also added to the horizontal stabilizer to improve lateral stability.

The first Beluga made its 5-hour, 21-minute maiden flight on September 13, 1994, and entered service with Airbus just over a year later. All the Guppies were replaced, on a one-for-one basis, by the end of 1998. In February 1999, SATIC awarded Sogerma a long-expected contract to build a fifth A300-600ST at Toulouse for delivery to Airbus at the end of 2000. At the same time, it also got a contract to provide on-line maintenance for the Beluga fleet in 1999 and began a "3C" check on the first aircraft.

The Beluga quickly began demonstrating its capabilities, which included almost twice the range and payload of the Super Guppy, and an increased cruise speed up to Mach 0.7. It also began to show dividends at the bottom line by almost halving the cost of transportation, which previously had amounted to up to 0.5 percent of the selling price of Guppy-era Airbus jetliners.

More important, it provided a long-term guarantee that the Airbus system of building complete, finished sections could continue. In this way, the Beluga ensured that each partner retained full responsibility for producing finished sections, rather than simply becoming a glorified component supplier. In the long term, the development of the Beluga underlined the determined spirit of Airbus and its continued efforts to unite European aerospace manufacturers in a way that until this time had never been possible.

INDEX